Harvard Business Review Guides

Arm yourself with the advice you need to succeed on the job, from the most trusted brand in business. Packed with how-to essentials from leading experts, the HBR Guides provide smart answers to your most pressing work challenges.

The titles include:

HBR Guide for Women at Work

HBR Guide to Being More Productive

HBR Guide to Better Business Writing

HBR Guide to Building Your Business Case

HBR Guide to Buying a Small Business

HBR Guide to Changing Your Career

HBR Guide to Coaching Employees

HBR Guide to Data Analytics Basics for Managers

HBR Guide to Dealing with Conflict

HBR Guide to Delivering Effective Feedback

HBR Guide to Emotional Intelligence

HBR Guide to Finance Basics for Managers

HBR Guide to Getting the Mentoring You Need

HBR Guide to Getting the Right Work Done

HBR Guide to Leading Teams

HBR Guide to Making Better Decisions

HBR Guide to Making Every Meeting Matter

HBR Guide to Managing Strategic Initiatives

HBR Guide to Managing Stress at Work

T0163845

HBR Guide to
Making Better Decisions

HBR Guide to **Making Better Decisions**

HARVARD BUSINESS REVIEW PRESS

Boston, Massachusetts

Copyright 2020 Harvard Business School Publishing Corporation

The web addresses referenced in this book were live and correct at the time of the book's publication but may be subject to change.

Library of Congress Cataloging-in-Publication Data

Title: HBR guide to making better decisions.
Other titles: Harvard Business Review guide to making better decisions | Harvard business review guides.
Description: Boston, Massachusetts : Harvard Business Review Press, [2020] | Series: Harvard Business Review guides | Includes index. |
Identifiers: LCCN 2019029435 | ISBN 9781633698154 (paperback) | ISBN 9781633698161 (ebook)
Subjects: LCSH: Decision making. | Problem solving. | Industrial management.
Classification: LCC HD30.23 .H388 2020 | DDC 658.4/03—dc23
LC record available at https://lccn.loc.gov/2019029435

ISBN: 978-1-63369-815-4
eISBN: 978-1-63369-816-1

The paper used in this publication meets the requirements of the American National Standard for Permanence of Paper for Publications and Documents in Libraries and Archives Z39.48-1992.

What You'll Learn

You're hiring a vendor, and out of the handful of candidates you're considering, you've narrowed it down to two. One can do the work fast, but at a high price tag. The other is cheaper, but would require a few additional weeks. Speed would certainly impress your boss, but the higher cost would use most of your budget. How do you decide?

You're faced with a litany of decisions at work every day—from hiring choices to prioritizing projects to making strategic decisions for your company. And even seemingly straightforward choices can be challenging. Unconscious biases, time pressure, and conflicting data can all add complexity to your decision-making processes, and it can be difficult to sort out how to make the right trade-offs and choose the best path forward.

But there are ways to improve the way you approach your toughest choices. This guide provides tips and tools to help you generate better ideas, evaluate your options more fairly, and make the final call, so you can come to the best decision more quickly and confidently—and ensure it sticks.

You'll learn how to:

- Avoid the psychological traps that can interfere with making smart choices

- Define clear decision-making roles for team members and stakeholders

- Ask questions to reframe your problem

- Generate ideas using top-down and bottom-up thinking

- Apply design thinking to your brainstorming process

- Balance data and intuition to narrow down alternatives

- Make appropriate trade-offs when comparing options

- Assess risk using a quantitative approach

- Decide confidently, even if you're short on time

- Overcome analysis paralysis

- Communicate your decision to stakeholders and be transparent about your process

- Respond productively when people second-guess your choice

- Correct course when you've made a mistake—and learn from it

Contents

Contents

Contents

Contents

SECTION FIVE

Managing Tough Situations

Introduction

You're tasked with creating a product that will bring new revenue streams to your company and also raise brand awareness within the market. Your team has come up with a few options and narrowed down the list to two: the first, a more advanced, higher-priced version of your staple product to encourage existing customers to buy the latest version of something they already love; and the second, a new, untested product type that will allow your company to enter new markets.

Building off of a trusted product may feel like the safer choice. The higher price point will result in more revenue, and you already have an established customer base. The new product, though, could bring in additional customers and provide opportunities for publicity, raising brand awareness. Of course, you don't know how this item will actually perform, since it has no past history of sales or customer feedback. If the product fails, it could reflect poorly on you and your team. Which opportunity do you choose?

Decisions like these are commonplace in day-to-day work. Whether selecting new hires, deciding on strategic plans of action, or even choosing what to order for a lunch meeting, you're constantly making decisions large and small. And they never seem to get any easier. The pressure to choose correctly and quickly—all while making important stakeholders happy—can stress even the most experienced executive, and understanding the potential consequences of your decisions can be increasingly difficult as uncertainty and competing priorities fog your view.

The good news is you can improve your decision-making skills so you find better solutions to your toughest problems, in a timely manner. This book provides practical advice to help you think more carefully about your decision-making process. It walks you through three key steps—generating options, evaluating your alternatives, and making your choice—and provides an array of tools and approaches to help you decide what works for you, your company, and any stakeholders.

Why Decision Making Is So Hard

In theory, making decisions should be straightforward: list your options, consider the data, choose the best one. But in reality, it's never that simple.

While data, analysis, and projections can certainly help with your decisions, many times they don't lead to clear-cut answers. Data may help you understand past performance and what certain alternatives offer, but you may discover that two options don't offer comparable trade-offs. Risk and uncertainty in future predictions mean you can't know for sure whether your choice is the right one. And evaluating data takes time and can slow down your decision making. If you're under time pressure, you may feel the need to skip careful analysis in favor of a gut reaction or your intuition.

Your emotions can also cause you to choose badly. The fear of failure, excitement about a project, eagerness to prove yourself, and the stress of stakeholders demanding an answer can all color the way you see a situation and lead you to make misinformed choices. Add in the tension and frustration of a team that just can't reach a consensus, and you have more than enough to keep you from making fair, impartial decisions.

You also may have habits and unconscious biases that misguide you. Mental shortcuts called *heuristics* can ensnare you, causing you to choose in favor of past experience or the status quo, for instance, rather than enabling you to look forward toward the best option. Psychological traps like these include feeling stuck because of the time and money you've already invested; moving forward too quickly because you're overconfident about your decision; or anchoring to the first idea you hear.

Finally, your decision-making processes can lead to subpar outcomes, right from the start. The way you frame a problem can limit or skew your thinking. In your search for data, you may only be seeking information that confirms your beliefs, rather than actively looking for evidence that counters them. And when decisions fall into gray areas—those places where data alone can't guide your choice—you may find yourself frozen with indecision, rather than taking a smart approach to using your judgment.

Fortunately, there are ways to overcome each of these issues. By becoming aware of the habits and behaviors that mislead you or hold you back, and by applying the right strategic approaches to your process, you can train yourself and your team to make smarter choices.

What This Book Will Do

This guide aims to help you improve the way you decide. It focuses on three key steps of the process: generating solutions, evaluating your options, and making the choice and following through. In each section, you'll find advice from researchers, practitioners, consultants, and other experts on how to make better decisions.

Getting started

The first section lays the groundwork for the decision-making process. First, you'll learn about the psychological traps that can cloud your judgment. By understanding these unconscious pitfalls—and how you can avoid them—you can have a clearer mind as you move toward making your toughest calls. The next chapter explains how to identify roles and responsibilities for everyone involved in the decision-making process: How the choice will be made, who the key players will be, who will implement the selected plan of action—and most importantly, who has the final say.

The final chapter in this section provides a seven-step checklist to counteract your biases. By following each step, you'll establish regular best practices, so you're consistently making better choices and reducing the time each decision takes.

Generate possible solutions

Before you can make a decision, you need options—sometimes a lot of them—and section 2 provides a variety of ways to generate these ideas. The first chapter describes the traditional brainstorming process in detail. The next chapter turns this process on its head, asking you to instead think of questions, which allows you to reframe the problem and look at it in different ways. Then, you'll learn about BrainSwarming, a technique where you consider both goals and resources to come up with potential solutions.

The last two chapters in the section challenge you to change the way you think so you can generate more creative alternatives. Chapter 7 asks you to think like a designer, using four tenets of design thinking—question, care, connect, and commit—to come up with fresh approaches to your most challenging issues. And the final chapter in this section forces you to break out of your usual ways of thinking, encouraging you to think about what you *could* do, rather than what is expected of you, to find novel solutions.

Evaluate your options

Idea generation may be a fun, open process of discovery, but soon you'll have to shift to a more difficult part of the decision-making process: narrowing down the list of options you've just come up with. Section 3 explains how to evaluate each of your alternatives, considering data, trade-offs, risk, and your own judgment.

The section begins with a recommendation: When evaluating ideas, look at them together, rather than one at a time. Doing so will provide you with better points of comparison between options. The next two chapters describe approaches to consider as you weigh alternatives against each other, including the pros-and-cons list and the even swaps method for evaluating trade-offs. From there, chapter 12 encourages you to become more strategic with the data you use for your decision. Rather than simply demanding more and more numbers, make your data search more disciplined by defining what you really need to make an informed choice.

While these approaches can help you consider options fairly by looking at the information you have, sometimes your data alone may not reveal the best path forward. Chapter 13 describes a process first used in the U.S. military in World War II to aid in quantifying risk with a set of questions about each alternative. Following this, Harvard Business School professor Joseph Badaracco presents five questions to ask yourself when you're navigating the gray areas where there is no clear answer. And finally, the last chapter in this section helps you understand when you should follow your gut—and when your intuition may lead you astray.

Make the choice and follow through

Once you've narrowed down your options, it's time to decide. Section 4 guides you through this process as you make the call, communicate your decision to others, and ensure that you don't second-guess yourself.

Many people worry that they'll make the wrong decision, but as executive coach Ed Batista says in chapter 16, you should worry less about making the right choice and worry more about ensuring the choice you've made turns out right. Following this, chapter 17 helps you overcome indecision by considering some simple questions and by putting the right organizational processes in place.

Of course, decisions mean nothing if they aren't implemented. For a decision to stick, you need to communicate your choice to stakeholders. Chapters 18 and 19 explain how to share your decision with those who need to know, as well as how to explain your process, so they accept your choice and consider it fair. But even the best-laid plans can have some resistance. Chapter 20 explains how to respond to those who question your decision. And in the final chapter of this section, you'll learn how to overcome your own hesitations, so you can stop worrying about whether you made the right choice.

Managing tough situations

Even after following these best practices, you may discover that your decision-making process runs into some common obstacles. In the final section of the book, you'll learn how to overcome some especially difficult scenarios. (If you're facing any of these situations now, you may find it useful to flip directly to this section.)

What do you do when you have a team that often can't reach an agreement? That's the question posed in the first chapter of this section. By establishing in advance how the choice will be made, you can alleviate any team-based conflict. And what if you're facing two bad options? While few decisions are simple, when faced with two especially bad alternatives, you can find yourself stuck. Chapter 23 explains how to overcome the uncertainty with such difficult calls and mitigate the damage, especially if the choice could negatively impact other people. And how should you react if, despite your best efforts, you make a wrong decision? Chapter 24 walks you through how to respond to this situation, not by ignoring your mistake, but by acting to correct the problem, learning from your misstep, and sharing what you've learned with others.

Sometimes, you just need to decide quickly. In the last chapter, psychologist, speaker, and author Nick Tasler provides a simple three-step framework for making any choice, no matter the amount of time you have. Whether you have five minutes or five months, this approach can work for you.

We all face challenging decisions, but the way we go about making these choices doesn't have to be difficult. By following the advice in this book, you can sidestep the psychological traps, sort through relevant information, and navigate uncertainty to arrive at the best option.

Getting Started

CHAPTER 1

The Hidden Traps in Decision Making

by John S. Hammond, Ralph L. Keeney, and Howard Raiffa

Making decisions is the most important job of any executive. It's also the toughest and the riskiest. Bad decisions can damage a business and a career, sometimes irreparably. So where do bad decisions come from? In many cases, they can be traced back to the way the decisions were made—the alternatives were not clearly defined, the right information was not collected, the costs and benefits were not accurately weighed. But sometimes the fault lies not in the decision-making process but rather in the mind of the decision maker. The way the human brain works can sabotage our decisions.

Reprinted from *Harvard Business Review*, January 2006, originally published September–October 1998 (product #R0601K).

Researchers have been studying the way our minds function in making decisions for half a century. This research, in the laboratory and in the field, has revealed that we use unconscious routines to cope with the complexity inherent in most decisions. These routines, known as *heuristics*, serve us well in most situations. In judging distance, for example, our minds frequently rely on a heuristic that equates clarity with proximity. The clearer an object appears, the closer we judge it to be. The fuzzier it appears, the farther away we assume it must be. This simple mental shortcut helps us to make the continuous stream of distance judgments required to navigate the world.

Yet, like most heuristics, it is not foolproof. On days that are hazier than normal, our eyes will tend to trick our minds into thinking that things are more distant than they actually are. Because the resulting distortion poses few dangers for most of us, we can safely ignore it. For airline pilots, though, the distortion can be catastrophic. That's why pilots are trained to use objective measures of distance in addition to their vision.

Researchers have identified a whole series of such flaws in the way we think in making decisions. Some, like the heuristic for clarity, are sensory misperceptions. Others take the form of biases. Others appear simply as irrational anomalies in our thinking. What makes all these traps so dangerous is their invisibility. Because they are hardwired into our thinking process, we fail to recognize them—even as we fall right into them.

For executives, whose success hinges on the many day-to-day decisions they make or approve, the psychological traps are especially dangerous. They can undermine everything from new-product development to acquisition and divestiture strategy to succession planning. While no one can rid his or her mind of these ingrained flaws, anyone can follow the lead of airline pilots and learn to understand the traps and compensate for them.

In this article, we examine a number of well-documented psychological traps that are particularly likely to undermine business decisions. In addition to reviewing the causes and manifestations of these traps, we offer some specific ways managers can guard against them. It's important to remember, though, that the best defense is always awareness. Executives who attempt to familiarize themselves with these traps and the diverse forms they take will be better able to ensure that the decisions they make are sound and that the recommendations proposed by subordinates or associates are reliable.

The Anchoring Trap

How would you answer these two questions?

Is the population of Turkey greater than 35 million?

What's your best estimate of Turkey's population?

If you're like most people, the figure of 35 million cited in the first question (a figure we chose arbitrarily) influenced your answer to the second question. Over the years, we've posed those questions to many groups of people. In half the cases, we used 35 million in the first question; in the other half, we used 100 million. Without fail, the answers to the second question increase by many millions when the larger figure is used in the first question. This simple test illustrates the common and often pernicious mental phenomenon known as *anchoring*. When considering a decision, the mind gives disproportionate weight to the first information it receives. Initial impressions, estimates, or data anchor subsequent thoughts and judgments.

Anchors take many guises. They can be as simple and seemingly innocuous as a comment offered by a colleague or a statistic appearing in the morning newspaper. They can be as insidious as a stereotype about a person's skin color, accent, or dress. In business, one of the most common types of anchors is a past event or trend. A marketer attempting to project the sales of a product for the coming year often begins by looking at the sales volumes for past years. The old numbers become anchors, which the forecaster then adjusts based on other factors. This approach, while it may lead to a reasonably accurate estimate, tends to give too much weight to past events and not enough weight to other factors. In situations characterized by rapid changes in the marketplace, historical anchors can lead to poor forecasts and, in turn, misguided choices.

Because anchors can establish the terms on which a decision will be made, they are often used as a bargaining tactic by savvy negotiators. Consider the experience of a large consulting firm that was searching for new office space in San Francisco. Working with a commercial real-estate broker, the firm's partners identified a building that met all their criteria, and they set up a meeting with the building's owners. The owners opened the meeting by laying out the terms of a proposed contract:

a ten-year lease; an initial monthly price of $2.50 per square foot; annual price increases at the prevailing inflation rate; all interior improvements to be the tenant's responsibility; an option for the tenant to extend the lease for ten additional years under the same terms. Although the price was at the high end of current market rates, the consultants made a relatively modest counteroffer. They proposed an initial price in the midrange of market rates and asked the owners to share in the renovation expenses, but they accepted all the other terms. The consultants could have been much more aggressive and creative in their counterproposal—reducing the initial price to the low end of market rates, adjusting rates biennially rather than annually, putting a cap on the increases, defining different terms for extending the lease, and so forth—but their thinking was guided by the owners' initial proposal. The consultants had fallen into the anchoring trap, and as a result, they ended up paying a lot more for the space than they had to.

What can you do about it?

The effect of anchors in decision making has been documented in thousands of experiments. Anchors influence the decisions not only of managers, but also of accountants and engineers, bankers and lawyers, consultants and stock analysts. No one can avoid their influence; they're just too widespread. But managers who are aware of the dangers of anchors can reduce their impact by using the following techniques:

- Always view a problem from different perspectives. Try using alternative starting points and approaches rather than sticking with the first line of thought that occurs to you.

- Think about the problem on your own before consulting others to avoid becoming anchored by their ideas.

- Be open-minded. Seek information and opinions from a variety of people to widen your frame of reference and to push your mind in fresh directions.

- Be careful to avoid anchoring your advisers, consultants, and others from whom you solicit information and counsel. Tell them as little as possible about your own ideas, estimates, and tentative decisions. If you reveal too much, your own preconceptions may simply come back to you.

- Be particularly wary of anchors in negotiations. Think through your position before any negotiation begins in order to avoid being anchored by the other party's initial proposal. At the same time, look for opportunities to use anchors to your own advantage—if you're the seller, for example, suggest a high, but defensible, price as an opening gambit.

The Status-Quo Trap

We all like to believe that we make decisions rationally and objectively. But the fact is, we all carry biases, and those biases influence the choices we make. Decision makers display, for example, a strong bias toward alternatives that perpetuate the status quo. On a broad scale, we can see this tendency whenever a radically new product is introduced. The first automobiles, revealingly called "horseless carriages," looked very much like the buggies they replaced. The first "electronic newspapers" appearing on the World Wide Web looked very much like their print precursors.

On a more familiar level, you may have succumbed to this bias in your personal financial decisions. People sometimes, for example, inherit shares of stock that they would never have bought themselves. Although it would be a straightforward, inexpensive proposition to sell those shares and put the money into a different investment, a surprising number of people don't sell. They find the status quo comfortable, and they avoid taking action that would upset it. "Maybe I'll rethink it later," they say. But "later" is usually never.

The source of the status-quo trap lies deep within our psyches, in our desire to protect our egos from damage. Breaking from the status quo means taking action, and when we take action, we take responsibility, thus opening ourselves to criticism and to regret. Not surprisingly, we naturally look for reasons to do nothing. Sticking with the status quo represents, in most cases, the safer course because it puts us at less psychological risk.

Many experiments have shown the magnetic attraction of the status quo. In one, a group of people were randomly given one of two gifts of approximately the same value—half received a mug, the other half a Swiss chocolate bar. They were then told that they could easily exchange the gift they received for the other gift. While you might expect that about half would have wanted to make the exchange, only one in ten actually did. The status quo exerted its power even though it had been arbitrarily established only minutes before.

Other experiments have shown that the more choices you are given, the more pull the status quo has. More people will, for instance, choose the status quo when there are two alternatives to it rather than one: A and B instead of just A. Why? Choosing between A and B requires additional effort; selecting the status quo avoids that effort.

In business, where sins of commission (doing something) tend to be punished much more severely than sins of omission (doing nothing), the status quo holds a particularly strong attraction. Many mergers, for example, founder because the acquiring company avoids taking swift action to impose a new, more appropriate management structure on the acquired company. "Let's not rock the boat right now," the typical reasoning goes. "Let's wait until the situation stabilizes." But as time passes, the existing structure becomes more entrenched, and altering it becomes harder, not easier. Having failed to seize the occasion when change would have been expected, management finds itself stuck with the status quo.

What can you do about it?

First of all, remember that in any given decision, maintaining the status quo may indeed be the best choice, but you don't want to choose it just because it is comfortable. Once you become aware of the status-quo trap, you can use these techniques to lessen its pull:

- Always remind yourself of your objectives and examine how they would be served by the status quo. You may find that elements of the current situation act as barriers to your goals.

- Never think of the status quo as your only alternative. Identify other options and use them as counterbalances, carefully evaluating all the pluses and minuses.

- Ask yourself whether you would choose the status-quo alternative if, in fact, it weren't the status quo.

- Avoid exaggerating the effort or cost involved in switching from the status quo.

- Remember that the desirability of the status quo will change over time. When comparing alternatives, always evaluate them in terms of the future as well as the present.

- If you have several alternatives that are superior to the status quo, don't default to the status quo just because you're having a hard time picking the best alternative. Force yourself to choose.

The Sunk-Cost Trap

Another of our deep-seated biases is to make choices in a way that justifies past choices, even when the past choices no longer seem valid. Most of us have fallen into this trap. We may have refused, for example, to sell a stock or a mutual fund at a loss, forgoing other, more attractive investments. Or we may have poured enormous effort into improving the performance of an employee whom we knew we shouldn't have hired in the first place. Our past decisions become what economists term *sunk costs*—old investments of time or money that are now irrecoverable. We know, rationally, that sunk costs are irrelevant to the present decision, but nevertheless they prey on our minds, leading us to make inappropriate decisions.

Why can't people free themselves from past decisions? Frequently, it's because they are unwilling, consciously or not, to admit to a mistake. Acknowledging a poor decision in one's personal life may be purely a private matter, involving only one's self-esteem, but in business, a bad decision is often a very public matter, inviting critical comments from colleagues or bosses. If you fire a poor performer whom you hired, you're making a public admission of poor judgment. It seems psychologically safer to let him or her stay on, even though that choice only compounds the error.

The sunk-cost bias shows up with disturbing regularity in banking, where it can have particularly dire consequences. When a borrower's business runs into trouble, a lender will often advance additional funds in hopes of providing the business with some breathing room to recover. If the business does have a good chance of coming back, that's a wise investment. Otherwise, it's just throwing good money after bad.

One of us helped a major U.S. bank recover after it made many bad loans to foreign businesses. We found that the bankers responsible for originating the problem loans were far more likely to advance additional funds—

repeatedly, in many cases—than were bankers who took over the accounts after the original loans were made. Too often, the original bankers' strategy—and loans—ended in failure. Having been trapped by an escalation of commitment, they had tried, consciously or unconsciously, to protect their earlier, flawed decisions. They had fallen victim to the sunk-cost bias. The bank finally solved the problem by instituting a policy requiring that a loan be immediately reassigned to another banker as soon as any problem arose. The new banker was able to take a fresh, unbiased look at the merit of offering more funds.

Sometimes a corporate culture reinforces the sunk-cost trap. If the penalties for making a decision that leads to an unfavorable outcome are overly severe, managers will be motivated to let failed projects drag on endlessly—in the vain hope that they'll somehow be able to transform them into successes. Executives should recognize that, in an uncertain world where unforeseeable events are common, good decisions can sometimes lead to bad outcomes. By acknowledging that some good ideas will end in failure, executives will encourage people to cut their losses rather than let them mount.

What can you do about it?

For all decisions with a history, you will need to make a conscious effort to set aside any sunk costs—whether psychological or economic—that will muddy your thinking about the choice at hand. Try these techniques:

- Seek out and listen carefully to the views of people who were uninvolved with the earlier decisions and who are hence unlikely to be committed to them.

- Examine why admitting to an earlier mistake distresses you. If the problem lies in your own wounded self-esteem, deal with it head-on. Remind yourself that even smart choices can have bad consequences, through no fault of the original decision maker, and that even the best and most experienced managers are not immune to errors in judgment. Remember the wise words of Warren Buffett: "When you find yourself in a hole, the best thing you can do is stop digging."

- Be on the lookout for the influence of sunk-cost biases in the decisions and recommendations made by your subordinates. Reassign responsibilities when necessary.

- Don't cultivate a failure-fearing culture that leads employees to perpetuate their mistakes. In rewarding people, look at the quality of their decision making (taking into account what was known at the time their decisions were made), not just the quality of the outcomes.

The Confirming-Evidence Trap

Imagine that you're the president of a successful mid-size U.S. manufacturer considering whether to call off a planned plant expansion. For a while you've been concerned that your company won't be able to sustain the rapid pace of growth of its exports. You fear that the value of the U.S. dollar will strengthen in coming months, making your goods more costly for overseas consumers and dampening demand. But before you put the brakes on the plant expansion, you decide to call up an acquaintance, the chief executive of a similar company that recently mothballed a new factory, to check her reasoning. She presents a strong case that other currencies are about to weaken significantly against the dollar. What do you do?

You'd better not let that conversation be the clincher, because you've probably just fallen victim to the confirming-evidence bias. This bias leads us to seek out information that supports our existing instinct or point of view while avoiding information that contradicts it. What, after all, did you expect your acquaintance to give, other than a strong argument in favor of her own decision? The confirming-evidence bias not only affects where we go to collect evidence but also how we interpret the evidence we do receive, leading us to give too much weight to supporting information and too little to conflicting information.

In one psychological study of this phenomenon, two groups—one opposed to and one supporting capital punishment—each read two reports of carefully conducted research on the effectiveness of the death penalty as a deterrent to crime. One report concluded that the death penalty was effective; the other concluded it was not. Despite being exposed to solid scientific information supporting counterarguments, the members of both groups became even more convinced of the validity of their own position after reading both reports. They automatically accepted the supporting information and dismissed the conflicting information.

There are two fundamental psychological forces at work here. The first is our tendency to subconsciously decide what we want to do before we figure out why we want to do it. The second is our inclination to be more engaged by things we like than by things we dislike—a tendency well documented even in babies. Naturally, then, we are drawn to information that supports our subconscious leanings.

What can you do about it?

It's not that you shouldn't make the choice you're subconsciously drawn to. It's just that you want to be sure it's the smart choice. You need to put it to the test. Here's how:

- Always check to see whether you are examining all the evidence with equal rigor. Avoid the tendency to accept confirming evidence without question.

- Get someone you respect to play devil's advocate, to argue against the decision you're contemplating. Better yet, build the counterarguments yourself. What's the strongest reason to do something else? The second strongest reason? The third? Consider the position with an open mind.

- Be honest with yourself about your motives. Are you really gathering information to help you make a smart choice, or are you just looking for evidence confirming what you think you'd like to do?

- In seeking the advice of others, don't ask leading questions that invite confirming evidence. And if you find that an adviser always seems to support your point of view, find a new adviser. Don't surround yourself with yes-men.

The Framing Trap

The first step in making a decision is to frame the question. It's also one of the most dangerous steps. The way a problem is framed can profoundly influence the choices you make. In a case involving automobile insurance, for example, framing made a $200 million difference. To reduce insurance costs, two neighboring states, New Jersey and Pennsylvania, made similar changes in their laws. Each state gave drivers a new option: By accepting a limited right to sue, they could lower their premiums. But the two states framed the choice in very different ways: In New Jersey, you automatically got the limited right to sue unless you specified otherwise; in Pennsylvania, you got the full right to sue unless you specified otherwise. The different frames established different status quos, and, not surprisingly, most consumers defaulted to the status quo. As a result, in New Jersey about 80% of drivers chose the limited right to sue, but in Pennsylvania only 25% chose it. Because of the way it framed the choice, Pennsylvania failed to gain approximately $200 million in expected insurance and litigation savings.

The framing trap can take many forms, and as the insurance example shows, it is often closely related to other psychological traps. A frame can establish the status quo or introduce an anchor. It can highlight sunk costs or lead you toward confirming evidence. Decision researchers have documented two types of frames that distort decision making with particular frequency:

Frames as gains versus losses

In a study patterned after a classic experiment by decision researchers Daniel Kahneman and Amos Tversky, one of us posed the following problem to a group of insurance professionals:

You are a marine property adjuster charged with minimizing the loss of cargo on three insured barges that sank yesterday off the coast of Alaska. Each barge holds $200,000 worth of cargo, which will be lost if not salvaged within 72 hours. The owner of a local marine-salvage company gives you two options, both of which will cost the same:

Plan A: *This plan will save the cargo of one of the three barges, worth $200,000.*

Plan B: *This plan has a one-third probability of saving the cargo on all three barges, worth $600,000, but has a two-thirds probability of saving nothing.*

Which plan would you choose?

If you are like 71% of the respondents in the study, you chose the "less risky" Plan A, which will save one barge for sure. Another group in the study, however, was asked to choose between alternatives C and D:

Plan C: *This plan will result in the loss of two of the three cargoes, worth $400,000.*

Plan D: *This plan has a two-thirds probability of resulting in the loss of all three cargoes and the entire $600,000 but has a one-third probability of losing no cargo.*

Faced with this choice, 80% of these respondents preferred Plan D.

The pairs of alternatives are, of course, precisely equivalent—Plan A is the same as Plan C, and Plan B is the same as Plan D—they've just been framed in different ways. The strikingly different responses reveal that people are risk averse when a problem is posed in terms of gains (barges saved) but risk seeking when a problem is posed in terms of avoiding losses (barges lost). Furthermore, they tend to adopt the frame as it is presented to them rather than restating the problem in their own way.

Framing with different reference points

The same problem can also elicit very different responses when frames use different reference points. Let's say you have $2,000 in your checking account and you are asked the following question:

Would you accept a fifty-fifty chance of either losing $300 or winning $500?

Would you accept the chance? What if you were asked this question:

Would you prefer to keep your checking account balance of $2,000 or to accept a fifty-fifty chance of having either $1,700 or $2,500 in your account?

Once again, the two questions pose the same problem. While your answers to both questions should, rationally speaking, be the same, studies have shown that many people would refuse the fifty-fifty chance in the first question but accept it in the second. Their different reactions result from the different reference points presented in the two frames. The first frame, with its reference point of zero, emphasizes incremental gains and losses, and the thought of losing triggers a conservative response in many people's minds. The second frame, with its reference point of $2,000, puts things into perspective by emphasizing the real financial impact of the decision.

What can you do about it?

A poorly framed problem can undermine even the best-considered decision. But any adverse effect of framing can be limited by taking the following precautions:

- Don't automatically accept the initial frame, whether it was formulated by you or by someone else. Always try to reframe the problem in various ways. Look for distortions caused by the frames.

- Try posing problems in a neutral, redundant way that combines gains and losses or embraces different reference points. For example: Would you accept a fifty-fifty chance of either losing $300, resulting in a bank balance of $1,700, or winning $500, resulting in a bank balance of $2,500?

- Think hard throughout your decision-making process about the framing of the problem. At points throughout the process, particularly near the end, ask yourself how your thinking might change if the framing changed.

- When others recommend decisions, examine the way they framed the problem. Challenge them with different frames.

The Estimating and Forecasting Traps

Most of us are adept at making estimates about time, distance, weight, and volume. That's because we're constantly making judgments about these variables and getting quick feedback about the accuracy of those judgments. Through daily practice, our minds become finely calibrated.

Making estimates or forecasts about uncertain events, however, is a different matter. While managers continually make such estimates and forecasts, they rarely get clear feedback about their accuracy. If you judge, for example, that the likelihood of the price of oil falling to less than $15 a barrel one year hence is about 40% and the price does indeed fall to that level, you can't tell whether you were right or wrong about the probability you estimated. The only way to gauge your accuracy would be to keep track of many, many similar judgments to see if, after the fact, the events you thought had a 40% chance of occurring actually did occur 40% of the time. That would require a great deal of data, carefully tracked over a long period of time. Weather forecasters and bookmakers have the opportunities and incentives to maintain such records, but the rest of us don't. As a result, our minds never become calibrated for making estimates in the face of uncertainty.

All of the traps we've discussed so far can influence the way we make decisions when confronted with uncertainty. But there's another set of traps that can have a particularly distorting effect in uncertain situations because they cloud our ability to assess probabilities. Let's look at three of the most common of these uncertainty traps:

The overconfidence trap

Even though most of us are not very good at making estimates or forecasts, we actually tend to be overconfident about our accuracy. That can lead to errors in judgment and, in turn, bad decisions. In one series of tests, people were asked to forecast the next week's closing value for the Dow Jones Industrial Average. To account for uncertainty, they were then asked to estimate a range within which the closing value would likely fall. In picking the top number of the range, they were asked to choose a high estimate they thought had only a 1% chance of being exceeded by the closing value. Similarly, for the bottom end, they were told to pick a low estimate for which they thought there would be only a 1% chance of the closing value falling below it. If they were good at judging their forecasting accuracy, you'd expect the participants to be wrong only about 2% of the time. But hundreds of tests have shown that the actual Dow Jones averages fell outside the forecast ranges 20% to 30% of the time. Overly confident about the accuracy of their predictions, most people set too narrow a range of possibilities.

Think of the implications for business decisions, in which major initiatives and investments often hinge on ranges of estimates. If managers underestimate the high end or overestimate the low end of a crucial variable, they may miss attractive opportunities or expose themselves to far greater risk than they realize. Much money has been wasted on ill-fated product-development projects because managers did not accurately account for the possibility of market failure.

The prudence trap

Another trap for forecasters takes the form of overcautiousness, or prudence. When faced with high-stakes decisions, we tend to adjust our estimates or forecasts "just to be on the safe side." Many years ago, for example, one of the Big Three U.S. automakers was deciding how many of a new-model car to produce in anticipation of its busiest sales season. The market-planning department, responsible for the decision, asked other departments to supply forecasts of key variables such as anticipated sales, dealer inventories, competitor actions, and costs. Knowing the purpose of the estimates, each department slanted its forecast to favor building more cars—"just to be safe." But the market planners took the numbers at face value and then made their own "just to be safe" adjustments. Not surprisingly, the number of cars produced far exceeded demand, and the company took six months to sell off the surplus, resorting in the end to promotional pricing.

Policy makers have gone so far as to codify overcautiousness in formal decision procedures. An extreme example is the methodology of "worst-case analysis," which was once popular in the design of weapons systems and is still used in certain engineering and regulatory settings. Using this approach, engineers designed weapons to operate under the worst possible combination of circumstances, even though the odds of those circumstances actually coming to pass were infinitesimal. Worst-case analysis added enormous costs with no practical benefit (in fact, it often backfired by touching off an arms race), proving that too much prudence can sometimes be as dangerous as too little.

The recallability trap

Even if we are neither overly confident nor unduly prudent, we can still fall into a trap when making estimates or forecasts. Because we frequently base our predictions about future events on our memory of past events, we can be overly influenced by dramatic events—those that leave a strong impression on our memory. We all, for example, exaggerate the probability of rare but catastrophic occurrences such as plane crashes because they get disproportionate attention in the media. A dramatic or traumatic event in your own life can also distort your thinking. You will assign a higher probability to traffic accidents if you have passed one on the way to work, and you will assign a higher chance of someday dying of cancer yourself if a close friend has died of the disease.

In fact, anything that distorts your ability to recall events in a balanced way will distort your probability assessments. In one experiment, lists of well-known men and women were read to different groups of people.

Unbeknownst to the subjects, each list had an equal number of men and women, but on some lists the men were more famous than the women while on others the women were more famous. Afterward, the participants were asked to estimate the percentages of men and women on each list. Those who had heard the list with the more famous men thought there were more men on the list, while those who had heard the one with the more famous women thought there were more women.

Corporate lawyers often get caught in the recallability trap when defending liability suits. Their decisions about whether to settle a claim or take it to court usually hinge on their assessments of the possible outcomes of a trial. Because the media tend to aggressively publicize massive damage awards (while ignoring other, far more common trial outcomes), lawyers can overestimate the probability of a large award for the plaintiff. As a result, they offer larger settlements than are actually warranted.

What can you do about it?

The best way to avoid the estimating and forecasting traps is to take a very disciplined approach to making forecasts and judging probabilities. For each of the three traps, some additional precautions can be taken:

- To reduce the effects of overconfidence in making estimates, always start by considering the extremes, the low and high ends of the possible range of values. This will help you avoid being anchored by an initial estimate. Then challenge your estimates of the extremes. Try to imagine circumstances where the actual figure would fall below your low or above your high, and adjust your range accordingly. Challenge the estimates of your subordinates and advisers in a similar fashion. They're also susceptible to overconfidence.

- To avoid the prudence trap, always state your estimates honestly and explain to anyone who will be using them that they have not been adjusted. Emphasize the need for honest input to anyone who will be supplying you with estimates. Test estimates over a reasonable range to assess their impact. Take a second look at the more sensitive estimates.

- To minimize the distortion caused by variations in recallability, carefully examine all your assumptions to ensure they're not unduly influenced by your memory. Get actual statistics whenever possible. Try not to be guided by impressions.

Forewarned Is Forearmed

When it comes to business decisions, there's rarely such a thing as a no-brainer. Our brains are always at work, sometimes, unfortunately, in ways that hinder rather than help us. At every stage of the decision-making process, misperceptions, biases, and other tricks of the mind can influence the choices we make. Highly complex and important decisions are the most prone to distortion because they tend to involve the most assumptions, the most estimates, and the most inputs from the most people. The higher the stakes, the higher the risk of being caught in a psychological trap.

The traps we've reviewed can all work in isolation. But, even more dangerous, they can work in concert, amplifying one another. A dramatic first impression might anchor our thinking, and then we might selectively seek out confirming evidence to justify our initial inclination. We make a hasty decision, and that decision establishes a new status quo. As our sunk costs mount, we become trapped, unable to find a propitious time to seek out a new and possibly better course. The psychological miscues cascade, making it harder and harder to choose wisely.

As we said at the outset, the best protection against all psychological traps—in isolation or in combination—is awareness. Forewarned is forearmed. Even if you can't eradicate the distortions ingrained into the way your mind works, you can build tests and disciplines into your decision-making process that can uncover errors in thinking before they become errors in judgment. And taking action to understand and avoid psychological traps can have the added benefit of increasing your confidence in the choices you make.

John S. Hammond is a consultant on decision making and a former professor at Harvard Business School in Boston. **Ralph L. Keeney** is a professor at Duke University's Fuqua School of Business in Durham, North Carolina. **Howard Raiffa** is the Frank Plumpton Ramsey Professor of Managerial Economics (Emeritus) at Harvard Business School. They are the coauthors of *Smart Choices: A Practical Guide to Making Better Decisions* (Harvard Business Review Press, 2015).

CHAPTER 2

Who Has the D?: How Clear Decision Roles Enhance Organizational Performance

by Paul Rogers and Marcia Blenko

IDEA IN BRIEF

Decisions are the coin of the realm in business. Every success, every mishap, every opportunity seized or missed stems from a decision someone made—or failed

Adapted from "Who Has the D?: How Clear Decision Roles Enhance Organizational Performance," *Harvard Business Review*, January 2006 (product #R0601D).

to make. Yet in many firms, decisions routinely stall inside the organization—hurting the entire company's performance.

The culprit? Ambiguity over who's accountable for which decisions. In one auto manufacturer that was missing milestones for rolling out new models, marketers *and* product developers each thought they were responsible for deciding new models' standard features and colors. Result? Conflict over who had final say, endless revisiting of decisions—and missed deadlines that led to lost sales.

How to clarify decision accountability? Assign clear roles for the decisions that most affect your firm's performance—such as which markets to enter, where to allocate capital, and how to drive product innovation. Think "RAPID":

- Who should **r**ecommend a course of action on a key decision?

- Who must **a**gree to a recommendation before it can move forward?

- Who will **p**erform the actions needed to implement the decision?

- Whose **i**nput is needed to determine the proposal's feasibility?

- Who **d**ecides—brings the decision to closure and commits the organization to implement it?

When you clarify decision roles, you make the right choices—swiftly and effectively.

IDEA IN PRACTICE

The RAPID Decision Model

For every strategic decision, assign the following roles and responsibilities:

People who . . .	Are responsible for . . .
Recommend	• Making a proposal on a key decision, gathering input, and providing data and analysis to make a sensible choice in a timely fashion • Consulting with input providers—hearing and incorporating their views, and winning their buy-in
Agree	• Negotiating a modified proposal with the recommender if they have concerns about the original proposal • Escalating unresolved issues to the decider if the "A" or "R" can't resolve differences • If necessary, exercising veto power over the recommendation
Perform	• Executing a decision once it's made • Seeing that the decision is implemented promptly and effectively
Input	• Providing relevant facts to the recommender that shed light on the proposal's feasibility and practical implications
Decide	• Serving as the single point of accountability • Bringing the decision to closure by resolving any impasse in the decision-making process • Committing the organization to implementing the decision

Decision-Role Pitfalls

In assigning decision roles:

- Ensure that only one person "has the D." If two or more people think they're in charge of a particular decision, a tug-of-war results.

- Watch for a proliferation of "A's." Too many people with veto power can paralyze recommenders. If many people must agree, you probably haven't pushed decisions down far enough in your organization.

- Avoid assigning too many "I's." When many people give input, at least some of them aren't making meaningful contributions.

The RAPID Model in Action

Example: At British department-store chain John Lewis, company buyers wanted to increase sales and reduce complexity by offering fewer salt and pepper mill models. The company launched the streamlined product set without involving the sales staff. And sales fell. Upon visiting the stores, buyers saw that salespeople (not understanding the strategy behind the recommendation) had halved shelf space to match the reduction in product range, rather than maintaining the same space but stocking more of the products.

To fix the problem, the company "gave buyers the D" on how much space product categories would have. Sales staff "had the A": If space allocations didn't make sense to them, they could force additional negotiations. They also "had the P," implementing product layouts in stores.

Once decision roles were clarified, sales of salt and pepper mills exceeded original levels.

Paul Rogers is a partner who leads Bain's London office; he formerly led Bain's Global Organization Practice. **Marcia Blenko** leads Bain & Company's Global Organization Practice and is a partner in the firm's Boston office. They are coauthors of *Decide and Deliver: Five Steps to Breakthrough Performance in Your Organization* (Harvard Business Review Press, 2010).

CHAPTER 3

A Checklist for Making Faster, Better Decisions

by Erik Larson

Managers make about three billion decisions each year, and almost all of them can be made better. The stakes for doing so are real: Decisions are the most powerful tool managers have for getting things done. While a tool like setting goals is aspirational, making decisions actually drives action. People usually do what they decide to do.

The good news is that there are ways to consistently make better decisions by using practices and technologies based on behavioral economics. In a three-month

Adapted from content posted on hbr.org, March 7, 2016 (product #H02PR2).

study of 100 managers, we found that managers who made decisions using best practices achieved their expected results 90% of the time, and 40% of them exceeded expectations. Other studies have shown that effective decision-making practices increase the number of good business decisions sixfold and cut failure rates nearly in half.[1]

But although there's great potential for using best practices to improve decision making, many organizations are not doing it. In a study of 500 managers and executives, we found that only 2% regularly apply best practices when making decisions, and few companies have systems in place to measure and improve decision making over time.

There are three reasons why this gap between potential and practice exists:

- **History.** Decision making in business has long been more art than science. That is partly because, until recently, most managers had relatively little access to accurate information. Few decision tools are widely used; the pros-and-cons list, popularized by Benjamin Franklin, is probably the most common—and it's nearly 250 years old. And then there is the unfortunate circumstance that economics in the twentieth century was based on the theory that people make rational choices when given good information, a theory proved to be somewhere between spotty and completely wrong, thanks to a revolution in behavioral economics led by Nobel Prize–winner Daniel Kahneman.

- **Psychology.** We are predictably irrational. Behavioral economists have uncovered a range of mental shortcuts and cognitive biases that distort our perceptions and hide better choices from us. Most business decisions are collaborative, which means groupthink and consensus work to compound our individual biases. Further, most business decisions are made under the stress of high uncertainty, so we often rely on gut feelings and intuition to reduce our mental discomfort. Decisions are hard work; there is a strong emotional impetus to just make them and move on.

- **Technology.** Enterprise software has automated many managerial tasks over the past 40 years. That shift has formed a foundation for better decision making, but it leaves the job unfinished. Behavioral economics shows that providing more complex and ambiguous information does little to help managers and their teams with the main challenges they must overcome to make better decisions. As a result, businesses can't see dramatic improvements in decision making by simply implementing more big data analytics software from the likes of SAP, Oracle, IBM, and Salesforce.

So what can managers do?

During product development of Cloverpop, our cloud solution for applying behavioral economics to decision making, we performed hundreds of experiments with tens of thousands of decision makers. We found that the most successful decision-making approach boils down to a simple checklist. But it's important to note that understanding the items in the list is not enough; this checklist must be *used* to be effective, since our biases don't go away just because we know they are there.

Each time you face a decision, use these steps as a tool to counteract your biases:

1. **Write down five preexisting company goals or priorities that the decision will impact.** Focusing on what is important will help you avoid the rationalization trap of making up reasons for your choices after the fact.

2. **Write down at least three, but ideally four or more, realistic alternatives.** It might take a little effort and creativity, but no other practice improves decisions more than expanding your choices.

3. **Write down the most important information you are missing.** You risk ignoring what you don't know because you are distracted by what you *do* know, especially in today's information-rich businesses.

4. **Write down the impact your decision will have one year in the future.** Telling a brief story of the expected outcome of the decision will help you identify similar scenarios that can provide useful perspective.

5. **Involve a team of at least two but no more than six stakeholders.** Getting more perspectives

reduces your bias and increases buy-in, but bigger groups have diminishing returns. According to research by Marcia Blenko, Michael Mankins, and Paul Rogers of Bain & Company, once you've reached seven people in your group, each additional member reduces decision effectiveness by 10%.[2]

6. **Write down what was decided, as well as why and how much the team supports the decision.** Doing so increases commitment and establishes a basis to measure the results of the decision.

7. **Schedule a decision follow-up in one to two months.** We often forget to check in when decisions are going poorly, missing the opportunity to make corrections and learn from what's happened.

Our research has found that managers who regularly follow these seven steps save an average of 10 hours of discussion, decide 10 days faster, and improve the outcomes of their decisions by 20%.

We need a new, scalable approach to managing decision performance. It must replace the historical theory of rational choice. It must acknowledge that our psychology often leads us astray. And it must use simple, friendly tools like this one, designed to have an outsize impact on how managers and teams make decisions.

Erik Larson is founder and CEO of Cloverpop, a cloud solution that applies behavioral economics and collaboration to help businesspeople make better decisions together. He is a graduate of MIT and Harvard Business School, a decorated U.S. Air Force officer, and an experienced technology executive based in San Francisco. Follow him on Twitter @erikdlarson.

NOTES

1. Chip Heath and Dan Heath, *Decisive: How to Make Better Choices in Life and Work* (New York: Crown Business, 2013).

2. Marcia W. Blenko, Michael C. Mankins, and Paul Rogers, *Decide and Deliver: Five Steps to Breakthrough Performance in Your Organization* (Boston: Harvard Business Review Press, 2010).

Generate Possible Solutions

CHAPTER 4

Idea Generation: The Basics

To make an informed decision, you need options. Alternatives are those options. After weighing the merits of a variety of alternatives, you will be in a better position to make the best decision for a given situation. In the absence of options, people are faced only with a yes-or-no question: Should we do this or not? That's not much of a choice, and it rarely produces an effective decision.

What you want are alternatives that represent a range of possibilities, even if your team must actively produce them. How are ideas generated?

Consider the example of George, a marketing manager at a consumer products company. George and his team are looking for ways to increase laundry detergent

---

Adapted from *Harvard Business Essentials: Decision Making* (product #7618), Harvard Business School Press, 2006.

sales in Latin America, as sales are 23% below what they had anticipated a year before, when they first entered the market. George gathers his team, asking for suggestions. After some silence, George suggests they consider changing the current packaging. Following his cue, Sofia chimes in with her own reflections about packaging and consumer trends. Another person then describes the packaging of a product that has sold particularly well in Latin America.

Everyone seems to have ideas to offer about packaging and how a change there might improve sales. The meeting concludes with the creation of a task force to research new packaging options.

Is a change in packaging the best solution for this company? Possibly. A task force charged with finding new packaging options might produce something of real value. But given the problem of disappointing Latin American sales, there may be alternative solutions of even greater value—for example, a change in pricing or a different approach to advertising and promotion. Perhaps the product itself should be altered in some tangible way. However, George and his team will never know the merits of these other solutions if they immediately take the packaging route. What went wrong?

In this scenario, George did not successfully engage the team in generating alternatives. He didn't promote healthy debate and constructive conflict. Instead, excessive group harmony resulted in a single-minded pursuit of the first idea that emerged: to investigate packaging options. There was little creativity or innovative thinking. As a result, no new ideas surfaced, and the group settled on the first alternative suggested, which had been the manager's idea.

As a decision maker, your goal at this stage is to identify as many alternatives as possible. Brainstorming is a common way to generate various ideas and courses of action.

Brainstorming

Brainstorming is a technique used to generate alternatives and problem solutions. It can be done by individuals, but it works better in groups because the insights and experiences of many people almost always produce more ideas than a person working alone, no matter how brilliant that person might be.

Begin with a blank flip chart page or a clean whiteboard. Ask people to suggest any ideas that come into their heads, or ask individuals to take a few minutes to develop their own lists of ideas to share publicly. Either way, record those ideas, but don't discuss their merits or allow criticism—at least not yet.

If you are leading the session, be scrupulously neutral as you recognize each contribution. Don't do anything that would signal your like or dislike of any of the alternatives presented. For example, avoid statements like these: "Thank you, Marta—that's the best idea we've heard all morning" or "Thanks, Rakesh. I doubt if that option is feasible, but I'll add it to the list." Comments like these can prejudice people for or against ideas even before discussing their merits. Neutrality is essential when the brainstorming leader has substantial influence over the group.

Brainstorming works best when people feel comfortable in speaking their minds, especially when their ideas conflict with those of their peers or their boss (see the sidebar "Tips for Generating Alternatives"). The atmosphere must also encourage introverted people to participate. We know from experience that there are some people who naturally speak up in group sessions. They tend to be outgoing and assertive, and they can easily dominate the discussion. But being outgoing and assertive doesn't correlate with having superior ideas. The person sitting silently at the far end of the table may have the best idea of the group. If you're leading the session, it's your job to elicit her ideas.

In this instance, it may be useful to ask people to write down their ideas and pass them to the session leader, rather than voicing them out loud. A creative problem solver who happens to be quiet in a group setting may have no trouble articulating ideas in written form.

Encourage open, candid dialogue by making it clear at the outset that the final outcome is not predetermined and everyone's input will be valued. Suggest that people think outside their individual or departmental roles. They should focus on what is best for the company, using all the available information.

When participants are unable to brainstorm any further, look at the list you've written down on the flip chart. How many ideas are there? If you have many options, it may be possible to group some under common themes. For example, the detergent company team might group its alternatives for boosting sales under these headings: packaging, pricing, retail displays, special promotions,

TIPS FOR GENERATING ALTERNATIVES

When you meet to generate alternative choices, follow these tips.

- Invite outsiders, experts as well as novices, to participate periodically in your meetings. Outsiders provide fresh ideas, a different perspective, and meaningful critiques.

- Conduct external benchmarking to observe how other companies and other industries address problems that are similar to yours.

- Encourage team members to step out of their traditional roles when generating alternatives. For example, if you're trying to brainstorm new product ideas, invite someone from your marketing group to participate, but ask that person to think about ideas from a financial perspective. You will probably find that more creative options surface when people think without their functional hats on.

- Ask probing questions such as, "What alternatives should we consider?" and "How should we respond to concerns about _____?" In this way, you avoid deciding too early on a solution that may not be the best one. Among the most important probing questions are those that test the validity of the group's assumptions.

(continued)

TIPS FOR GENERATING ALTERNATIVES

Those assumptions should be made explicit and discussed openly. (To read more about asking questions, flip to the next chapter.)

- Be willing to consider and discuss views that differ from your own. This is not easy, and the group leader should be the model for this behavior. If the leader demonstrates tolerance for and interest in ideas contrary to her own, others may notice and follow suit.

- Revisit abandoned alternatives from time to time to ensure that they were discarded for sound reasons.

- Don't overlook hybrid alternatives. In many cases, it's possible to combine the best features of two or more existing ideas into a new and superior one. For example, hybrid cars bring together environmental fuel efficiency of electric power alongside the dependability of a standard gas engine. Even minivans that first appeared in the 1980s combined the most popular features of a boxy, trucklike van with the comforts of a passenger car.

and product reformulation. Grouping related ideas helps to focus the effort.

There is some evidence that you can get more out of brainstorming when ideas are generated independently and later brought into a group session in which people can share and build on their ideas. This technique prevents the immediate convergence of ideas—through persuasion or peer pressure—that normally occurs when people with different ideas begin talking to each other. There are plenty of opportunities for discussion and convergence later.

A wide variety of alternatives help you to make an informed decision. When you encourage team participation, facilitate creative conflict, and listen to ideas, you are likely to generate a full slate of options that will serve you well as you continue through the decision-making process.

CHAPTER 5

Better Brainstorming

by Hal Gregersen

About 20 years ago I was leading a brainstorming session in one of my MBA classes, and it was like wading through oatmeal. We were talking about something that many organizations struggle with: how to build a culture of equality in a male-dominated environment. Though it was an issue the students cared about, they clearly felt uninspired by the ideas they were generating. After a lot of discussion, the energy level in the room was approaching nil. Glancing at the clock, I resolved to at least give us a starting point for the next session.

"Everyone," I improvised, "let's forget about finding answers for today and just come up with some new

Reprinted from *Harvard Business Review*, March–April 2018 (product #R1802C).

questions we could be asking about this problem. Let's see how many we can write down in the time we have left." The students dutifully started to throw out questions, and I scribbled them on a chalkboard, redirecting anybody who started to suggest an answer. To my surprise, the room was quickly energized. At the end of the session, people left talking excitedly about a few of the questions that had emerged—those that challenged basic assumptions we had been making. For instance: Were there grassroots efforts we could support, rather than handing down rules from the top? And: What could we learn from pockets within our own organization that had achieved equality, instead of automatically looking elsewhere for best practices? Suddenly, there was much more to discuss, because we had opened up unexpected pathways to potential solutions.

Brainstorming for questions, not answers, wasn't something I'd tried before. It just occurred to me in that moment, probably because I had recently been reading sociologist Parker Palmer's early work about creative discovery through open, honest inquiry. But this technique worked so well with the students that I began experimenting with it in consulting engagements, and eventually it evolved into a methodology that I continue to refine. By now I've used it with hundreds of clients, including global teams at Chanel, Danone, Disney, EY, Fidelity, Genentech, Salesforce, and dozens of other companies; nonprofit organizations; and individual leaders I've coached.

Underlying the approach is a broader recognition that fresh questions often beget novel—even transformative—insights. Consider this example from the field of psychology: Before 1998 virtually all well-trained psychologists focused on attacking the roots of mental disorders and deficits, on the assumption that well-being came down to the absence of those negative conditions. But then Martin Seligman became president of the American Psychological Association, and he reframed things for his colleagues. What if, he asked in a speech at the APA's annual meeting, well-being is just as driven by the *presence* of certain *positive* conditions—keys to flourishing that could be recognized, measured, and cultivated? With that question, the positive psychology movement was born.

Brainstorming for questions rather than answers makes it easier to push past cognitive biases and venture into uncharted territory. We've seen this dynamic in academic studies—in social psychologist Adam Galinsky's research on the power of reframing during times of transition, for instance. Yet lingering in a questioning mode doesn't come naturally to most people, because we're conditioned from an early age to just keep the answers coming.

The methodology I've developed is essentially a process for recasting problems in valuable new ways. It helps people adopt a more creative habit of thinking and, when they're looking for breakthroughs, gives them a sense of control. There's actually something they can do other than sit and wait for a bolt from the blue. Here, I'll describe how and why this approach works. You can use it anytime you (in a group or individually) are feeling stuck or trying to imagine new possibilities. And if you make it a regular practice in your organization, it can foster a stronger culture of collective problem solving and truth seeking.

What Process Should We Follow?

Over the years I have tested variations of this brainstorming process—I now call it a "question burst"—and collected and analyzed participant data and feedback to gauge what works best. I've experimented with different group sizes, time allotments, and numbers of questions; impromptu versus scheduled sessions; various modes of capturing ideas; and greater and lesser amounts of coaching (on, for example, what constitutes a "good" question and how to make creative leaps in thinking). I've done temperature checks in sessions and conducted surveys after them, looking for the effects of each variation. Over time the question burst has settled into a standard format, which consists of three steps:

1. Set the stage

To begin, select a challenge you care deeply about. Perhaps you've suffered a setback or you have a vague sense of an intriguing opportunity. How do you know it's ripe for a breakthrough question? It's probably a good candidate if it "makes your heart beat fast," as Intuit's chairman and CEO, Brad Smith, put it to me. You'll give it your full attention and want to engage others in thinking about it.

Invite a few people to help you consider that challenge from fresh angles. Though you can do this exercise on your own, bringing others into the process will give you access to a wider knowledge base and help you maintain a constructive mindset. As Ned Hallowell says in *Driven to Distraction at Work* (which was based on his decades of research on how to sustain productive attention), worry "feasts on a solitary victim." When you ask others to participate in a question burst, you're making yourself vulnerable by sharing the problem—but you're also summoning empathy, which fosters idea generation, as we've learned from design thinking. And you engage others in the cause in a nonthreatening way.

It's best to include two or three people who have no direct experience with the problem and whose cognitive style or worldview is starkly different from yours. They will come up with surprising, compelling questions that you would not, because they have no practiced ways of thinking about the problem and no investment in the status quo. They're more likely to ask third-rail questions and point to elephants in the room—they don't know not to.

In traditional brainstorming—the kind that focuses on generating answers—individuals perform better than groups, on average. That's because powerful group dynamics such as "social loafing" (coasting on others' contributions) and social anxiety (fears about how one's ideas will be judged) can hinder original thinking and stifle the voices of introverted members. But the question burst methodology, by design, reverses many of those destructive dynamics by prompting people to depart from their usual habits of social interaction. For one thing, it creates a safe space for anyone, including a quieter person, to offer a different perspective. Because a question burst doesn't demand that anyone instantly assert a point of view, people often feel more comfortable speaking up. The sole focus on questions also suspends the automatic rush to provide an answer—and ultimately helps expand the problem space for deeper exploration.

Once you've gathered your partners for this exercise, give yourself just two minutes to lay out the problem for them. People often believe that their problems require detailed explanations, but quickly sharing the challenge forces you to frame it in a high-level way that doesn't constrain or direct the questioning. So just hit the highlights. Try to convey how things would change for the better if the problem were solved. And briefly say why you are stuck—why it hasn't already been solved.

This approach helped Odessa, a manager at a global financial services company, reframe what she initially viewed as a complex communications challenge: rolling out a new strategy to people performing different tasks at many levels across many geographies. She prefaced her question burst with a simple explanation, sharing her hopes for getting everyone "rowing in the same direction" and her frustration that one set of messages couldn't do the job, given employees' diverse roles and perspectives. By leaving it at that, she created room for a line of questioning that radically altered her understanding. She came to see this as a leadership challenge, not just an internal marketing campaign. If she could find a way to trust others to convey the strategy, she could mobilize a small army of managers in the field to tailor messages for maximum local impact.

Often, as I'm outlining the rules for a question burst, people ask what kinds of questions they should contribute—or how they can be confident that a question is a good one for further pursuit. While I hesitate to be definitive about this, it's true that not all questions have equal potential to lead to novel solutions. To up your odds, keep these principles in mind:

- Traditional divergent-thinking techniques (for example, making random associations or taking on an alternative persona) can help unlock new questions and, ultimately, new territory.

- Questions are most productive when they are open versus closed, short versus long, and simple versus complex.

- Descriptive questions (what's working? what's not? why?) best precede speculative ones (what if? what might be? why not?).

- Shifting from simple questions that require only recall to more cognitively complex ones that demand creative synthesis produces better breakthrough thinking.

- Questions are annoying and distracting when they don't spring from a deeply held conviction about what the group wants to achieve.

- Questions are toxic when they are posed aggressively, putting people on the spot, casting unwarranted doubt on their ideas, or cultivating a culture of fear.

Before opening the floor to your group, clearly spell out two critical rules: First, people can contribute only questions. Those who try to suggest solutions—or respond to others' questions—will be redirected by you, the convener of the session. And second, no preambles or justifications that frame a question will be allowed, because they'll guide listeners to see the problem in a certain way—the very thing you're trying to avoid.

You'll also want to do a quick emotion check up front. As the "owner" of the challenge, take a moment to reflect on it: Are your feelings about it positive, neutral, or negative? Jot down a few words that capture your own baseline mood. No need to spend more than 10 seconds on this. You'll do the same thing again after the session is over. These checks are important because emotions affect creative energy. The exercise's objective is not only to spark valuable new questions but also to provide an emotional boost that will make you more likely to follow up on them.

Here I should point out that your creative energy will ebb and flow in the coming days, weeks, and months— and preparing yourself for that is critical. Transformational ideas start out as exhilarating but turn vexing as unforeseen snags reveal themselves. Then they settle into hard work that, with luck, produces moments of hope that will see the change through. If you expect that turbulence from the beginning, you'll be better able to ride it out later.

2. Brainstorm the questions

Now set a timer and spend the next four minutes collectively generating as many questions as possible about the challenge. As in all brainstorming, don't allow pushback on anyone's contributions. The more surprising and provocative the questions are, the better.

When working with large enterprises, I often notice that senior leaders in particular find it excruciatingly difficult to resist offering answers—even for four minutes—when people start throwing out questions. At one manufacturing company, for instance, when questions about supply chain issues started bubbling up, the group's leader couldn't help jumping in to display his knowledge. This impulse is understandable, and not just for senior executives. In a hierarchy, any manager's failure to have ready answers may be perceived as an embarrassing stumble. Questions, especially counterintuitive ones, make many of us feel so uncomfortable that we hasten to utter any default response that buys us time to recover. But when we're feeling blocked on a problem, answering questions this way is a waste of time. After all, the reason we're hung up is that our go-to answers aren't getting us anywhere.

In this exercise the emphasis is on quantity. By asking the group to generate as many questions as possible in the time allotted—try for at least 15—you'll keep them short, simple, and fresh. Write every question down verbatim on paper, a laptop, or a tablet instead of on a whiteboard so that you can capture everything accurately. And ask group members to keep you honest afterward. Otherwise you might commit unconscious censoring that repels lines of inquiry you don't immediately understand or want to hear.

As you're recording, add your own questions to the mix. That will often reveal patterns in how you have habitually framed a problem (and might have unknowingly perpetuated it).

Is there some magic about precisely four minutes and 15 questions? No, but the time pressure helps participants stick to the "questions only" rule. Any effort spent on answers will mean less chance of hitting the goal. People will also be more likely to generate questions that are unburdened by qualifications and assumptions, and they'll find it easier to resist explaining why they're asking any question that might seem to come from left field. Even better, studies show that moderate performance pressures can enhance creative output.

Moreover, perhaps because selective sustained attention places real demands on the human brain, energy often wanes in this exercise after three and a half minutes, especially for beginners. And as a practical matter, transcribing dozens of questions can turn into an onerous task. For both those reasons, it's better to use multiple question bursts to reshape, refine, and ultimately solve a challenge than to cram too much activity into one longer session.

Once the timer goes off, do a second quick emotional check. How do you feel about the challenge now? (And how do others in the group feel about it?) Are you more positive than you were four minutes ago? If not, and if the setting allows, maybe rerun the exercise. Or get some rest and try again tomorrow. Or try it with some different people. Research has established that creative problem solving flourishes when people work in positive emotional states. After poring over survey data from more than 1,500 global leaders, I'm convinced that part of the power of the question burst lies in its ability to alter a person's view of the challenge, by dislodging—for most—that feeling of being stuck.

3. Identify a quest—and commit to it

On your own, study the questions you jotted down, looking for those that suggest new pathways. About 80% of the time, this exercise produces at least one question that usefully reframes the problem and provides a new angle for solving it. Select a few that intrigue you, strike you as different from how you've been going about things, or even cause you to feel a bit uncomfortable.

Now try expanding those few into their own sets of related or follow-on questions. A classic way of doing this is the "five whys" sequence developed by Toyota Industries' founder, Sakichi Toyoda—or the variation on it suggested by Stanford's Michael Ray in *The Highest Goal*. Ask yourself why the question you chose seemed important or meaningful. Then ask why the reason you just gave is important—or why it's a sticking point. And so on. By better understanding why a question really matters and what obstacles you might face in addressing it, you deepen your resolve and ability to do something about it and further broaden the territory of possible solutions. In the case of Odessa, the manager with a strategy to roll out, one breakthrough question—Could you recruit field leaders to communicate it locally?—provoked other questions: Why haven't I done that in the past? Could I trust others to do this well? Why do I have a problem extending that trust?

Finally, commit to pursuing at least one new pathway you've glimpsed—and do so as a *truth seeker*. I steal that term from NASA engineer Adam Steltzner's account of working at the Jet Propulsion Laboratory, where the "right kind of crazy" people manage to accomplish things like landing a robotic rover on Mars. Set aside considerations of what might be more comfortable to conclude or easier to implement, and instead adopt an innovator's focus on the "job to be done" and what it will take to get the problem solved. Devise a near-term action plan: What concrete actions will you personally take in the next three weeks to find potential solutions suggested by your new questions?

After one question burst I helped facilitate, a chief marketing officer from a multidivisional company resolved to track down some facts. He had been wrestling with concerns about hypercompetitive behaviors in his business unit. In a question burst session he led with others, it dawned on him that he had been making a big assumption: that the founders of his division had chosen its unique compensation scheme to create a culture of internal rivalry. His to-do list started with getting on their calendars and asking them about this. Guess what? Not only was this not a culture they had aimed for, but they were dismayed to learn it existed. His meetings with them gave rise to a new emphasis on culture and values in the unit—and created the context in which the

CMO could intervene and address toxic behaviors. The point here is that arriving at assumption-challenging questions is essential but never sufficient. An action plan and follow-up can clarify the problem and break open the pathway to change.

How Can We Make It a Habit?

I usually recommend doing at least three rounds of the question burst exercise for a given issue. Although it's valuable as a one-off activity, the more you do it, the deeper you'll go in your thinking. After the leader of a development team at a global software company did the exercise repeatedly, she came to the realization that her original conception of a problem was "superficial." Through persistent questioning, she told me, she "arrived at a much more meaningful challenge to conquer."

Even with three rounds, the time investment is minimal. It's an efficient path to fresh perspectives and creativity. The process will also get easier the more you do it. When people crank up their questioning activity for the first time with this approach, it feels strange because it's out of line with established norms at work and in life. Since childhood, they've been conditioned not to ask questions.

James T. Dillon, an education professor emeritus at the University of California, Riverside, spent a career studying this phenomenon in classrooms. He was shocked by how rarely students asked questions—which are critical to learning. The problem wasn't a lack of curiosity. "Every time that conditions have been provided for them (not by a mere pause, 'Any questions?

No? OK, open your books'), a flood of intriguing student questions has poured forth," Dillon writes. When he surveyed other teachers about this, they almost universally agreed that "students indeed have questions but do not go on to ask them in class." Why not? They're afraid to do so, Dillon says, "largely because of their experience with negative reactions from the teacher (and from classmates)." They learn to keep their questions to themselves and to repeat back well-rehearsed answers when quizzed by their teachers, according to Tony Wagner, a senior fellow at the Learning Policy Institute. Other researchers—looking at arenas of human learning and interaction such as community forums, medical consultations, political institutions, and workplaces—have consistently come to the same conclusion: Questioning is an innate human behavior that's actively subverted and systematically shut down.

And power struggles don't help matters. In social groups, dominant individuals inevitably emerge; left unchecked, they find ways to build and perpetuate their power. One common way to do this is to silence questioners—those pesky curious minds whose queries might suggest that the leader hasn't quite figured it all out.

Of course, many business leaders, recognizing the imperative for constant innovation, do try to encourage questions. But their employees have already internalized the habit of not asking them—especially the tough ones. We need to change this habit. That's what my MIT colleague Robert Langer, the health care technology innovator who has been called the "Edison of medicine," has been doing with his students and postdocs. In a recent interview he said: "When you're a student, you're judged by how well you answer questions. Somebody else asks the questions, and if you give good answers, you'll get a good grade. But in life, you're judged by how good your questions are." As he mentors people, he explicitly focuses their attention on making this all-important transition, knowing "they'll become great professors, great entrepreneurs—great something—if they ask good questions."

Organizations can raise their questioning quotient in various ways. For example, in my field experience, I've found that people become better questioners in environments where they're encouraged to value creative friction in everyday work. At companies like Amazon, ASOS, IDEO, Patagonia, Pixar, Tesla, and Zappos, for example, people often come together to tackle challenges by asking one another tough questions—in hallways, lunchrooms, or even conference rooms. Research by management professors Andrew Hargadon of UC Davis and Beth Bechky of NYU shows that those volunteering ideas in such companies do not mindlessly spit back answers to the questions posed; they respectfully build on the comments and actions of others, considering "not only the original question but also whether there is a better question to be asked." As they do this over and over, new solutions emerge.

People also become better questioners in organizational cultures where they feel safe doggedly pursuing the truth, no matter where it takes them. To create such cultures, MIT's Ed Schein says, leaders must show humility, vulnerability, and trust, and they must empower others and treat them equitably. When those conditions aren't present, questions tend to be constrained or, worse, crushed.

Interestingly, when I've facilitated question bursts with very large groups (broken down into subgroups of three to six people), I have noticed that the people least likely to engage in the exercise and follow the rules are the folks with the highest positions or greatest technical expertise. Whether they feel they're above the exercise or worry that sharing problems will make them appear incompetent, they cripple the truth-seeking capability of the entire group as others watch them disengage or scoff at contributions. If that's the example and tone leaders are setting in a single microcosmic exercise, imagine the dampening impact they have on inquiry throughout their organizations.

Finally, people must hold themselves accountable for follow-up. Few things are more annoying than a colleague who *only* asks questions. People must take responsibility for exploring the pathways those questions open up and discovering valuable answers. This is especially true for leaders. Everyone else is taking cues from them about when, where, how, and why the status quo should be challenged. They must carve out time to help gather and analyze newer, better, and different information. It's a sign of ownership when leaders go out of their way to do that. It shows others that management is committed to crafting a future where questions count.

Hal Gregersen is executive director of the MIT Leadership Center, a senior lecturer in leadership and innovation at the MIT Sloan School of Management, a Thinkers50 globally ranked management thinker, and the founder of the 4-24 Project. He is also the author of *Questions Are the Answer: A Breakthrough Approach to Your Most Vexing Problems at Work and in Life* and the coauthor of *The Innovator's DNA: Mastering the Five Skills of Disruptive Innovators.*

CHAPTER 6

BrainSwarming: A New Approach to Finding Solutions

by Tony McCaffrey

Brainstorming, the practice of sharing ideas while withholding judgment, rose to popularity in the early 1950s with the promise of producing more ideas. The problem is, it never worked as well as expected. No study has shown that brainstorming produces more alternatives than people just working alone for a while and then coming together to share their ideas and build on them. Sharing one idea at a time—via talking—is incredibly inefficient. Further, extroverts always dominate introverts

---

Adapted from "Brainswarming: Because Brainstorming Doesn't Work" (video), on hbr.org, March 24, 2014.

and hamper idea generation, even if you have a talented facilitator.

BrainSwarming, an approach I pioneered with my colleagues, directly challenges the foundation of brainstorming by asking, *Why do we need to talk in the first place?*[1] This concept is probably best explained using an example from the lives of insects. Ants solve problems by leaving signals in their environment that influence the behavior of their fellow ants. When searching for food, successful ants leave traces of pheromones along their trails, a signal to the other ants that there's a path to dinner.

If we make a problem-solving graph, then humans can quietly leave their signals—that is, their ideas—for others to build upon. In a BrainSwarming graph, the goal grows downward into refined subgoals. Resources interact together and grow upward, as shown in figure 6-1. When the two directions connect, solutions start to emerge.

FIGURE 6-1

How BrainSwarming works

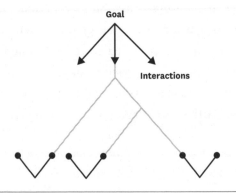

Let's see how brainstorming would handle a classic management problem, like this real-life conundrum at Pacific Power & Light. Winter storms in the Cascade Mountains leave power lines loaded with ice, which if left unattended will break the lines. Having workers climb the poles to shake the lines is both dangerous and time consuming. Managers searched for a better method for years. What if they had used BrainSwarming?

To start, they would simply place the goal at the top of the BrainSwarming graph and a few known resources at the bottom, as seen in figure 6-2. Then, the group would be instructed not to talk but to simply add sticky notes and drawn lines to the graph. People who are naturally top-down thinkers would start refining the goal. Other, naturally bottom-up thinkers would analyze how the resources could be used, or they would add new resources. Pretty soon, the two directions would connect, an indication that the group was finding ways to use the resources to solve the problem.

FIGURE 6-2

List goals and resources

Remove ice from power lines

●

●   ●   ●
Ladder   Workers   Poles

FIGURE 6-3

Solutions to power line problem

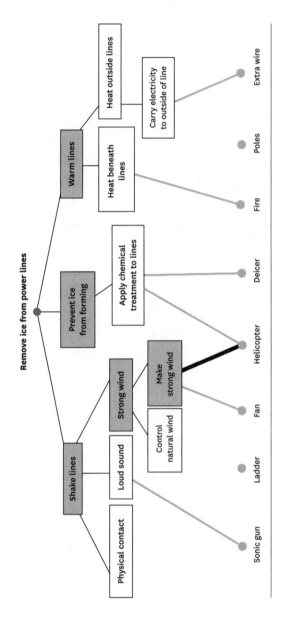

Figure 6-3 shows a careful refinement of the goal as well as Pacific Power & Light's actual solution of using a helicopter's downdraft to shake the lines enough to remove the ice. Other solutions are also shown, including using a helicopter to drop a deicing agent onto the lines and using the conducted electricity to generate enough heat to melt the ice on the outside of the lines.

We don't know for sure whether using BrainSwarming would have helped Pacific Power & Light come up with an effective solution more quickly. But our pilot work shows that BrainSwarming produces up to 115 ideas in 15 minutes versus 100 ideas per hour for traditional brainstorming. By switching from talking to writing on a structured graph, BrainSwarming greatly improves the effectiveness of group work.

Tony McCaffrey is the chief technology officer of Innovation Accelerator.

NOTE

1. BrainSwarming is a registered trademark of Dr. Tony McCaffrey.

CHAPTER 7

The Four Phases of Design Thinking

by Warren Berger

What can people in business learn from studying the ways successful designers solve problems and innovate? On the most basic level, they can learn to question, care, connect, and commit—four of the most important things successful designers do to achieve significant breakthroughs.

Having studied more than a hundred top designers in various fields over the past couple of years (while doing research for a book), I found that there were a few shared behaviors that seemed to be almost second nature to many designers. And these ingrained habits were intrinsically linked to the designer's ability to bring

---

Adapted from content posted on hbr.org, July 29, 2010.

original ideas into the world as successful innovations. All of which suggests that they merit a closer look.

Question

If you spend any time around designers, you quickly discover this about them: They ask, and raise, a lot of questions. Often this is the starting point in the design process, and it can have a profound influence on everything that follows. Many of the designers I studied, from Bruce Mau to Richard Saul Wurman to Paula Scher, talked about the importance of asking "stupid questions"—ones that challenge the existing realities and assumptions in a given industry or sector. The persistent tendency of designers to do this is captured in the joke designers tell about themselves: *How many designers does it take to change a light bulb? Answer: Does it have to be a light bulb?*

In a business setting, asking basic "why" questions can make the questioner seem naïve, while putting others on the defensive, as in, "What do you mean 'Why are we doing it this way?' We've been doing it this way for 22 years!" But by encouraging people to step back and reconsider old problems or entrenched practices, the designer can begin to reframe the challenge at hand, which can then steer thinking in new directions. For businesses in today's volatile marketplace, the ability to question and rethink basic fundamentals—What business are we really in? What do today's consumers actually need or expect from us?—has never been more important. (To read more about asking questions and reframing your problem, turn back to chapter 5.)

Care

It's easy for companies to say they care about customer needs. But to really empathize, you must be willing to do what many of the best designers do: Step out of the corporate bubble and immerse yourself in the daily lives of people you're trying to serve. What impressed me about design researchers such as Jane Fulton Suri, partner emeritus and executive design director of IDEO, was the dedication to really observing and paying close attention to people, because this is usually the best way to ferret out their deep, unarticulated needs. Focus groups and questionnaires don't cut it; designers know that you must care enough to actually be present in people's lives.

Connect

Designers, I discovered, have a knack for synthesizing, for taking existing elements or ideas and mashing them together in fresh new ways. This can be a valuable shortcut to innovation because it means you don't necessarily have to invent from scratch. By coming up with "smart recombinations" (to use a term coined by the designer John Thackara), Apple has produced some of its most successful hybrid products, and Nike has smartly combined a running shoe with an iPod to produce its groundbreaking NikePlus line, which enables users to program their runs.

It isn't easy to come up with these great combos. Designers know that you must "think laterally"—searching far and wide for ideas and influences—and must also be willing to try connecting ideas that might not seem to go together. Nondesigners can also embrace this way of thinking.

Commit

It's one thing to dream up original ideas. But designers quickly take those ideas beyond the realm of imagination by giving form to them. Whether a napkin sketch, a prototype carved from foam rubber, or a digital mock-up, the quick and rough models that designers constantly create are a critical component of innovation, because when you give form to an idea, you begin to make it real.

But it's also true that when you commit to an idea early—putting it out into the world while it's still young and imperfect—you increase the possibility of short-term failure. Designers tend to be much more comfortable with this risk than most of us. They know that innovation often involves an iterative process with setbacks along the way, and those small failures are actually useful because they show the designer what works and what needs fixing. The designer's ability to "fail forward" is a particularly valuable quality in times of dynamic change. Today, many companies find themselves operating in a test-and-learn business environment that requires rapid prototyping. Which is just one more reason to pay attention to the people who've been conducting their work this way all along.

———————

Warren Berger is author of the book *A More Beautiful Question: The Power of Inquiry to Spark Breakthrough Ideas*. Follow him on Twitter @GlimmerGuy.

CHAPTER 8

When Solving Problems, Think About What You Could Do, Not What You Should Do

by Francesca Gino

On a Saturday night in Modena, a picturesque city in one of the most well-known culinary regions of Italy, a couple and their two young sons dined at the Michelin three-star restaurant Osteria Francescana. The father

Adapted from content posted on hbr.org, April 27, 2018 (product #H04AWH).

ordered for the family "Tradition in Evolution," a tasting menu with 10 of the restaurant's most popular dishes. One of them, "snails under the earth," is served as a soup. Snails are covered by an "earth" of coffee, nuts, and black truffle, and "hidden" under a cream made with raw potato and garlic foam. As maître d' Giuseppe Palmieri took the order, he noticed a slightly desperate look on the boys' faces. Palmieri turned to the younger boy and asked, "What would *you* like to have?" He answered, "Pizza!"

Osteria Francescana is not the kind of place that offers pizza. Yet, without hesitation, Palmieri excused himself and called the city's best pizzeria. A taxi showed up not long after with the pizza, and Palmieri delivered it to the table. At many fancy restaurants, this would have been unthinkable. But the two children and their parents will likely never forget Palmieri's act of kindness. And, as Palmieri told me, "It simply took a change of course, and one pizza."

Nobody likes a troublemaker at work. We've all had colleagues who annoy us or deviate from the script with no heads-up, causing conflict or wasting time: jerks and show-offs who seem to be difficult for no good reason and people who break rules just for the sake of it and make others worse off in the process. But there are also people who know how to turn rule breaking into a contribution. Rebels like Palmieri deserve our respect and our attention, because they have a lot to teach us.

One of the biggest lessons is, if given a challenging situation—kids who want pizza—we all tend to default to what we *should* do instead of asking what we *could* do. My colleagues and I did an experiment in which I gave participants difficult ethical challenges where there seemed to be no good choice. I then asked participants either "What should you do?" or "What could you do?" We found that the "could" group were able to generate more creative solutions. Approaching problems with a "should" mindset gets us stuck on the trade-off the choice entails and narrows our thinking on one answer, the one that seems most obvious. But when we think in terms of "could," we stay open-minded, and the trade-offs involved inspire us to come up with creative solutions.

At work, of course, the "what could we do" person is also the one who is seen as slowing things down. "What if . . . ?" and "How about . . . ?" are questions that keep adding options to the discussion. But rebels understand that it's always worth resisting time pressure to give yourself a moment to reflect. Consider an extreme example: Captain Chesley B. "Sully" Sullenberger is the pilot of a USAirways jetliner that, shortly after taking off from New York's La Guardia Airport in January 2009, hit a flock of birds and lost both its engines. Sully had 155 people on board and very little time to find a place to land in a city of tall buildings. Most captains would have taken the most obvious course and tried to land at the nearest airport—likely with catastrophic results. Sully worked through the standard emergency procedures (what he *should* do), but also allowed himself to think about what he *could* do. He decided to put the plane down on the Hudson River, and everyone was saved.

Another problem people have with rebels at work is the conflict that sometimes results. Rebels are prone to disagreement. But some tension is a positive thing, because it can help get people to move past *should* to *could*. According to research by Li Huang and Adam D. Galinsky of Northwestern University, when we experience conflict, we generate more original solutions than when we are in a more cooperative mood. When there is tension, we also tend to scrutinize options and deeply explore alternatives, which leads to novel insights. Understanding this, Ariel Investments, a money management firm headquartered in Chicago, appoints a devil's advocate during meetings who is charged with poking holes. This served the firm well during the 2008 financial crisis. The approach helped the firm be thoughtful about the stocks it followed: One person who followed a particular stock would make a recommendation on buying or selling it; another would argue the opposite.

I have found in my own research, when people are asked to meet two goals that appear to be at odds, their ideas are more innovative. For example, my colleagues and I invited participants in one experiment to use limited supplies to build prototypes of different products in the laboratory. We told some of them to build novel products. We told others to build cheap products. And we told a third group to build a novel product but keep costs low. We then asked another group of people to evaluate all the products the three groups created on their originality. The products that received the highest scores were those created by people who had what appeared to be conflicting goals at the outset. Of course, conflict and disagreements can be taken too far. But making things harder can yield better results.

Osteria Francescana is a place where rule breaking is encouraged, right from the top. The chef and restaurant's owner Massimo Bottura does not fit the usual leader's mold: He is in the trenches, cleaning the street outside the restaurant first thing in the morning, helping with the prep of the staff meal, playing soccer with the staff between services, and unloading delivery trucks. He delights in challenging the conventions of Italian cooking. A century ago, boiling meats for the Italian dish *Bollito misto* (boiled mixed meats) was a practical choice, given limited cooking methods. Cooking the meat *sous vide*, as Bottura did, transformed the dish—which he calls *Bollito non bollito* (boiled meats, not boiled)—into one that's more flavorful and pleasing to the eye.

When other members of the staff see their leader do the unexpected, they embrace it as well. They know that they work in the kind of place where ordering a pizza for two desperate kids will not be looked down on. We can all learn from Palmieri. But we can also learn from the kind of place where he works—where rebels are made to feel at home.

Francesca Gino is a behavioral scientist and the Tandon Family Professor of Business Administration at Harvard Business School. She is the author of the books *Rebel Talent: Why It Pays to Break the Rules at Work and in Life* and *Sidetracked: Why Our Decisions Get Derailed, and How We Can Stick to the Plan*. Follow her on Twitter @francescagino.

Evaluate Your Options

CHAPTER 9

To Make Better Choices, Look at All Your Options Together

by Shankha Basu and Krishna Savani

We make thousands of decisions every day. Some are fairly simple—we decide when to wake up, what to have for breakfast, what to wear to work, which emails to reply to—while others are more complex, requiring us to weigh different options. For example, when buying a laptop, we want to compare different models to find the best one for our budget; when choosing a retirement

Adapted from content posted on hbr.org, June 28, 2017 (product #H03QYO).

plan, we compare options to find one with the highest returns for our risk appetite; and when hiring, we compare multiple applicants to identify the best candidate.

When faced with such decisions, we can examine one option at a time or review all our options together. For example, when deciding which job candidates to interview, a hiring manager may evaluate one candidate's résumé at a time, form an opinion about it, and then move on to assess the next one. Alternatively, she may lay out the résumés of all applicants on a table, evaluate and compare them, and then decide whom to interview. Similarly, an investor may view the details of one mutual fund at a time or visit a mutual fund comparison website. And a supply chain manager may consider information of the suppliers individually or view them together on a spreadsheet.

In a study published in the journal *Organizational Behavior and Human Decision Processes*, we examined how these two ways of evaluating options can influence people's choices. We recruited 2,783 research participants in the United States from an online panel (Amazon Mechanical Turk) and a university in Singapore. Across seven experiments, we asked the participants to make choices from options that were presented either sequentially or all at once. Some decisions were simple, such as which camera model to buy; others were complex decisions that a manager would make, such as which supplier to award a contract to. Overall, we found that people were, on average, 22% more likely to choose the objectively best option when they viewed options together rather than one at a time.

In the first experiment, we asked 201 online participants to choose different models of five types of electronic products (for example, laptop, microwave oven).
For each type of product, there were six models to choose
from, each with varying attributes. For example, for each
laptop model, we provided information about the pro-
cessor speed, RAM, storage capacity, battery life, and
warranty. The best option was the model with the highest value for these attributes.

We randomly selected half of the participants to view
options together. For each product, they viewed the information of all six models together on their screen
and then chose one. The other half of the participants
viewed the options one at a time—information about the
first model was displayed on the first screen, the second
model on the next, and so on. Once they viewed all the
models for a product, they could go back and forth between screens and choose one. We found that those who
viewed options individually chose the best option 75% of
the time, while those who viewed options together identified the best product 84% of the time.

In another experiment, we asked 472 online participants to imagine that they owned a restaurant and had
to order weekly supplies for five items, such as milk and
ketchup. For each product, the person had to choose
one of five different suppliers, each quoting a different
price for a given quantity of the product. For example,
participants could choose to buy milk from a supplier
selling 35 gallons for $73.50, another selling 29 gallons
for $69.60, and so on. We designed the options such that
there was always one supplier that had the lowest price

per unit of quantity but people would have to do some calculation to figure out which supplier that was. As in the previous experiment, half of the participants viewed all the suppliers for each product together and made a choice; the other half reviewed one supplier at a time and then made a choice. We found that participants who viewed options one at a time identified the cheapest supplier 55% of the time, whereas those who viewed the information together did so 61% of the time. We found the same pattern of results in another experiment, where we statistically controlled for people's math ability.

Why is it that people make better decisions when they view options all together rather than one at a time? One possibility is that with all the information in front of them, people can compare the options more thoroughly and can more easily identify the best one. But when people view options individually, they form an overall judgment about each one and then have to go back and compare.

We tested this possibility in another experiment, which used a setup similar to the previous two but also asked participants to write down the thoughts they had when making their choices. We used text analysis software called LIWC, which categorizes words into different classes, to analyze their written responses.

Once again we saw that people who viewed options together selected the best one more often than those who viewed options individually. We also found that compared with those who viewed options one at a time, people who viewed options together used more phrases suggesting deep thought (for example, "I *think* X is more than Y" or "*Hence,* I feel Y is the correct option"). This finding supports our assumption that people compare options more thoroughly when they view them all together.

But people don't always evaluate their options simultaneously. In a separate survey, we asked 211 online participants to recall some past decisions and report whether they generally viewed options together or one at a time. These participants reported that they viewed options sequentially in about half of the decisions they made.

Similarly, companies don't always help consumers look at their options all at once. In analyzing the websites of leading auto manufacturers and life insurance providers, we found that all websites had pages for individual products (allowing people to consider one product at a time), but only some websites allowed people to view multiple products together on the same screen. Most websites had a comparison tool, but it only allowed people to compare options on a few dimensions.

How we appraise and present options might seem to be a trivial matter. But our research indicates that it can have a real impact on the ultimate quality of our decisions.

Shankha Basu is a lecturer (assistant professor) of marketing at Leeds University Business School, University of Leeds, UK. **Krishna Savani** is the Provost's Chair in Business and director of the Culture Science Institute at Nanyang Business School, Nanyang Technological University, Singapore.

CHAPTER 10

The Pros and Cons of Pros-and-Cons Lists

by Chris Charyk

Pondering an important decision? Chances are that you will consider jotting down the pros and cons of your options. The pros-and-cons list enjoys a long and storied history, going back at least as far as 1772, when Benjamin Franklin advised his friend and fellow scientist Joseph Priestley to "divide half a sheet of paper by a line into two columns, writing over the one Pro, and over the other Con." But how useful is a pros-and-cons list, really? It's only fitting to consider the pros and cons of this popular decision-making tool.

Adapted from content posted on hbr.org, January 6, 2017 (product #H03E7T).

The Pros

Rigor

Making the effort to think through all possible pros and cons of a given course of action and then capturing them in writing minimizes the likelihood that you have missed critical factors. (The sidebar "Variables to Consider" provides a list of some of these criteria.) Assigning weights to each of the pros and cons is an additional exercise that promotes deeper thinking and presumably leads to better-quality decision making.

Emotional distance

Important decisions are likely to evoke powerful emotions. Going through the steps of creating a pros-and-cons list can create what researchers Ozlem Ayduk and Ethan Kross refer to as a "self-distanced perspective," in which the decision is viewed as an "external" problem to be addressed, easing the impact of the emotions surrounding the decision. Deferring the decision pending the pro-con analysis also provides a gap in time in which powerful emotions can dissipate, reducing the risk of an "amygdala hijack," the cognitive phenomenon popularized by Daniel Goleman's work on emotional intelligence, in which perceived emotional threats can lead to extreme actions, often with undesirable outcomes.

Familiarity and simplicity

Perhaps most compelling of all, the pros-and-cons list is generally well understood, requires no special computational or analytical expertise, and is elegantly simple to administer.

VARIABLES TO CONSIDER

Once you and your team have identified a set of alternatives, you must assess if each one is a viable option to solve your problem. There are a number of variables to keep in mind:

- **Costs.** How much will the alternative cost? Will it result in savings now or over the long term? Are there any hidden costs? Are there likely to be additional expenses down the road? Does this alternative fall within the budget?

- **Benefits.** What profits or other benefits will we realize if we implement a given alternative? Will it increase the quality of our product? Will customer satisfaction increase? Will it make our people more effective?

- **Financial impact.** How will the monetary costs and benefits of this option translate into bottom-line results as measured by net present value? What will be the timing of that result? Will implementation require us to borrow money?

- **Intangibles.** Will our reputation improve if we implement a given alternative? Will our customers or employees be more satisfied and loyal?

- **Time.** How long will it take to implement this idea? What is the probability of delays and the impact of such delays on the schedule?

(continued)

VARIABLES TO CONSIDER

- *Feasibility.* Can this alternative be executed realistically? Are there any obstacles that must be overcome? What resistance might be encountered inside or outside the organization?

- *Resources.* How many people are needed to implement each alternative? Are they available, or will we need to hire and train them? What other projects will suffer if individuals focus on this option?

- *Risk.* What risks are associated with this idea? Could it result in loss of profits or competitive advantage? How might competitors respond? What information would reduce these uncertainties? Would it be difficult and costly to obtain risk-reducing information?

- *Ethics.* Is this alternative legal? Is it in the best interests of customers, employees, and the community where we operate? Would we feel comfortable if other people knew that we were considering this option?

There is little doubt that your decisions must take into account these considerations. Obviously, some will be more important to your company than others.

Adapted from *Harvard Business Essentials: Decision Making* (product #7618), Harvard Business School Press, 2006.

The Cons

Vulnerable to cognitive biases

Cognitive biases are common patterns of thinking that have been demonstrated to lead to errors in judgment and poor decision making. Unfortunately, the same simplicity that makes a pros-and-cons list so appealing creates many opportunities for a host of cognitive biases to emerge, including:

- **The framing effect.** Pros-and-cons lists generally are about evaluating two alternatives: a "thumbs up or thumbs down" scenario and an example of "narrow framing," a bias created by overly constraining the set of possible outcomes.

- **The overconfidence effect.** A well-established cognitive bias is the tendency of individuals to overestimate the reliability of their judgments. When creating a pros-and-cons list, it is likely that many people assume a level of accuracy in their assessment of pros and cons that simply isn't there.

- **The illusion of control.** When faced with the task of envisioning possible outcomes, a common bias is to believe that one can control outcomes that in reality are not controllable.

Reliance on analytical thinking

Using an analytical tool such as a pros-and-cons list emphasizes the objective, "just the facts" side of decision making. Intuition, or what Goleman terms "direct knowing," has captured the attention of many brain science researchers. In one study, the "absence of attentive deliberation," AKA "go with your gut," was demonstrated to result in decisions with better outcomes than those derived from the use of analytical tools.[1]

The Verdict

My experience as an executive coach suggests that for the vast majority of decisions that my clients deem to be critical, a pros-and-cons list is useful *only* as a very high-level preliminary thinking aid. I believe this is because the decisions leaders most often bring to coaching are ones for which they perceive the stakes as being high—the client has strong positive or negative (or both) emotions associated with possible outcomes. And when the stakes are high, the potential interference of cognitive biases, wishful thinking, self-limiting beliefs, and similar barriers to objectivity rise. High-stakes decisions therefore require approaches that address these complications. Self-awareness, reflection, and actively applying a range of mindsets are examples of alternatives to the pros-and-cons list that shed light on these hidden, unconscious cognitive biases, ultimately leading to better insights and better decision outcomes.

Chris Charyk is an executive coach with The Boda Group, a leadership and team development firm.

NOTE

1. A. Dijksterhuis, M. W. Bos, L. F. Nordren, and R. B. van Baaren, "On Making the Right Choice: The Deliberation-Without-Attention Effect," *Science* 311, no. 5763 (2006): 1005–1007.

CHAPTER 11

Even Swaps: A Rational Method for Making Trade-Offs

by John S. Hammond, Ralph L. Keeney, and Howard Raiffa

Some decisions are easy. If you want to fly from New York to San Francisco as cheaply as possible, you simply find the airline offering the lowest fare and buy a ticket. You have only a single objective, so you need to make only a single set of comparisons. But having only one objective, as any decision maker knows, is a rare luxury.

Excerpted from *Harvard Business Review*, March–April 1998 (product #98206).

Usually, you're pursuing many different objectives simultaneously. Yes, you want a low fare, but you also want a convenient departure time, a direct flight, an aisle seat, and an airline with an outstanding safety record. And you'd like to earn frequent flyer miles in one of your existing accounts. Now the decision is considerably more complicated. You have to make trade-offs.

Making wise trade-offs is one of the most important and difficult challenges in decision making. The more alternatives you're considering and the more objectives you're pursuing, the more trade-offs you'll need to make. The sheer volume of trade-offs, though, is not what makes decision making so hard. It's the fact that each objective has its own basis of comparison. For one objective, you may compare the alternatives using precise numbers or percentages: 34%, 38%, 53%. For another objective, you may need to make broad relational judgments: high, low, medium. For another, you may use purely descriptive terms: yellow, orange, blue. You're not just trading off apples and oranges; you're trading off apples and oranges and elephants.

How do you make trade-offs when comparing such widely disparate things? In the past, decision makers have relied mostly on instinct, common sense, and guesswork. They've lacked a clear, rational, and easy-to-use trade-off methodology. To help fill that gap, we have developed a system—which we call *even swaps*—that provides a practical way of making trade-offs among any set of objectives across a range of alternatives. In essence, the even-swap method is a form of bartering—it forces you to think about the value of one objective in terms of another. How many frequent flyer miles, for example, would you sacrifice for a $50 reduction in airfare? How long would you delay your departure time to be assured an aisle seat? Once you have made such value judgments, you can make sense of the variety of different measurement systems. You have a solid, consistent basis for making sensible trade-offs.

The even-swap method will not make complex decisions easy; you'll still have to make hard choices about the values you set and the trades you make. What it does provide is a reliable mechanism for making trades and a coherent framework in which to make them. By simplifying and codifying the mechanical elements of trade-offs, the even-swap method lets you focus all your mental energy on the most important work of decision making: deciding the real value to you and your organization of different courses of action.

Creating a Consequences Table

Before you can begin making trade-offs, you need to have a clear picture of all your alternatives and their consequences for each of your objectives. A good way to create that picture is to draw up a *consequences table*. Using pencil and paper or a computer spreadsheet, list your objectives down the left side of a page and your alternatives along the top. This will give you an empty matrix. In each box of the matrix, write a concise description of the consequence that the given alternative (indicated by the column) will have for the given objective (indicated by the row). You'll likely describe some consequences in quantitative terms, using numbers, and others in qualitative terms, using words. The important thing is to use consistent terminology in describing all the consequences for a given objective; in other words, use consistent terms across each row. If you don't, you won't be able to make rational swaps between the objectives.

To illustrate what a consequences table actually looks like, let's examine one created by a young man we'll call Vincent Sahid. The only child of a widower, Vincent plans to take time off from college, where he's majoring in business, to help his father recover from a serious illness. To make ends meet while away from school, he will need to take a job. He wants a position that pays adequately, has good benefits and vacation allowances, and involves enjoyable work, but he'd also like to gain some experience that will be useful when he returns to school. And, given his dad's frail condition, it is very important that the job give him the flexibility to deal with emergencies. After a lot of hard work, Vincent identifies five possible jobs. Each has very different consequences for his objectives, and he charts those consequences in a consequences table. (See table 11-1.)

As we see, a consequences table puts a lot of information into a concise and orderly format that allows you to compare your alternatives easily, objective by objective. It gives you a clear framework for making trade-offs. Moreover, it imposes an important discipline, forcing you to define all alternatives, all objectives, and all relevant consequences at the outset of the decision process. Although a consequences table is not too hard to create, we're always surprised at how rarely decision makers take the time to put down on paper all the elements of a

TABLE 11-1

Sahid's consequences table

			ALTERNATIVES		
Objectives	**Job A**	**Job B**	**Job C**	**Job D**	**Job E**
Monthly salary ($)	2,000	2,400	1,800	1,900	2,200
Flexibility	Moderate	Low	High	Moderate	None
Business skills development	Computer	People management, computer	Operations, computer	Organization	Time management, multitasking
Annual vacation days	14	12	10	15	12
Benefits	Health, dental, retirement	Health, dental	Health	Health, retirement	Health, dental
Enjoyment	Great	Good	Good	Great	Boring

complex decision. Without a consequences table, important information can be overlooked and trade-offs can be made haphazardly, leading to wrongheaded decisions.

Eliminating "Dominated" Alternatives

Once you've defined and mapped the consequences of each alternative, you should always look for opportunities to eliminate one or more of the alternatives. The fewer the alternatives, the fewer trade-offs you'll ultimately need to make. To identify alternatives that can be eliminated, follow this simple rule: if alternative A is better than alternative B on some objectives and no worse than B on all other objectives, B can be eliminated from consideration. In such cases, B is said to be *dominated* by A—it has disadvantages without any advantages.

Say you want to take a relaxing weekend getaway. You have five places in mind, and you have three objectives: low cost, good weather, and short travel time. In looking at your options, you notice that alternative C costs more, has worse weather, and requires the same travel time as alternative D. Alternative C is dominated by D and therefore can be eliminated.

You need not be rigid in thinking about dominance. In making further comparisons among your options, you may find, for example, that alternative E also has higher costs and worse weather than alternative D but has a slight advantage in travel time—it would take half an hour less to get to E. You may easily conclude that the relatively small time advantage doesn't outweigh the weather and cost disadvantages. For practical purposes, alternative E is dominated—we call this *practical domi-nance*—and you can eliminate it as well. By looking for dominance, you have just made your decision much simpler—you only have to choose among three alternatives, not five.

A consequences table can be a great aid in identifying dominated alternatives. But if there are many alternatives and objectives, there can be so much information in the table that it gets hard to spot dominance. Glance back at Vincent Sahid's consequences table and you'll see what we mean. To make it easier to uncover dominance, you should create a second table in which the descriptions of consequences are replaced with simple rankings. Working row by row—that is, objective by objective—determine the consequence that best fulfills the objective and replace it with the number 1; then find the second-best consequence and replace it with the number 2; and continue in this way until you've ranked the consequences of all the alternatives. When Vincent looks at the vacation objective in his table, for example, he sees that 15 days ranks first, 14 days ranks second, the two 12 days tie for third, and 10 days ranks fifth. When he moves from the quantitatively measured objectives to the qualitatively measured ones, he finds that more thought is required because the rankings need to be based on subjective judgments rather than objective comparisons. In assessing the benefits packages, for example, he decides that dental coverage is more important to him than a retirement plan, and he makes his rankings on that basis. (See table 11-2.)

Dominance is much easier to see when you're looking at simple rankings. Vincent sees that Job E is clearly

TABLE 11-2

Sahid's ranking table

ALTERNATIVES

Objectives	Job A	Job B	Job C	Job D	Job E
Monthly salary	3	1	5	4	2
Flexibility	2 (tie)	4	1	2 (tie)	5
Business skills development	4	1	3	5	2
Annual vacation	2	3 (tie)	5	1	3 (tie)
Benefits	1	2 (tie)	5	4	2 (tie)
Enjoyment	1 (tie)	3 (tie)	3 (tie)	1 (tie)	5

dominated by Job B: it's worse on four objectives and equivalent on two. Comparing Job A and Job D, he sees that Job A is better on three objectives, tied on two, and worse on one (vacation). When an alternative has only one advantage over another, as with Job D, it is a candidate for elimination due to practical dominance. In this case, Vincent easily concludes that the one-day vacation advantage of Job D is far outweighed by its disadvantages in salary, business-skills development, and benefits. Hence, Job D is practically dominated by Job A and can also be eliminated.

Using a ranking table to eliminate dominated alternatives can save you a lot of effort. Sometimes, in fact, it can lead directly to the final decision. If all your alternatives but one are dominated, the remaining alternative is your best choice.

Making Even Swaps

Although it's possible that you'll be down to a single alternative at this point, it's far more likely that you'll still have a number of alternatives to choose from. Because none of the remaining alternatives are dominated, each will have some advantages and some disadvantages relative to each of the others. The challenge now is to make the right trade-offs between them. The even-swap method offers a way to even out the advantages and disadvantages systematically until you are left with a clear choice.

What do we mean by even swaps? To explain the concept, we need to state an obvious but fundamental tenet of decision making: If every alternative for a given objective is rated equally—for example, if they all cost the same—you can ignore that objective in making your decision. If all airlines charge the same fare for the New York to San Francisco flight, then cost doesn't matter. Your decision will hinge on only the remaining objectives.

The even-swap method provides a way to adjust the values of different alternatives' consequences in order to render them equivalent and thus irrelevant. As its name implies, an even swap increases the value of an alternative in terms of one objective while decreasing its value by an equivalent amount in terms of another objective. If, for example, American Airlines charged $100 more for a New York to San Francisco flight than did Continental, you might swap a $100 reduction in the American fare for 2,000 fewer American frequent-flyer miles. In other words, you'd "pay" 2,000 frequent flyer miles for the fare cut. Now American would score the same as Continental on the cost objective, so cost would have no bearing in deciding between them. Whereas the assessment of dominance enables you to eliminate alternatives, the even-swap method allows you to eliminate objectives. As more objectives are eliminated, fewer comparisons need to be made, and the decision becomes easier.

The even-swap method can be a powerful tool in business decision making. Imagine you're running a Brazilian cola company and several other companies have expressed interest in buying franchises to bottle and sell your product. Your company currently has a 20% share of its market, and it will earn $20 million in the fiscal year just ending. You have two key objectives for the coming year: increasing profits and expanding market share. You estimate that franchising would reduce your profits to $10 million due to start-up costs, but it would increase your share to 26%. If you don't franchise, your profits would rise to $25 million, but your share would increase only to 21%. You put this all down in a consequences table.

Which is the smart choice? As the table indicates, the decision boils down to whether the additional $15 million profit from not franchising is worth more or less than the additional 5% market share you would gain from franchising. To resolve that question, you can apply the even-swap method following a straightforward process.

First, determine the change necessary to cancel out an objective

If you could cancel out the $15 million profit advantage gained by not franchising, the decision would depend only on market share.

Second, assess what change in another objective would compensate for the needed change

You must determine what increase in market share would compensate for the profit decrease of $15 million. After a careful analysis of the long-term benefits of increased share, you determine that a 3% increase would make up for the lost $15 million.

Third, make the even swap

In the consequences table, you reduce the profit of the not-franchising alternative by $15 million while increasing its market share by 3%. The restated consequences (a $10 million profit and a 24% market share) are equivalent in value to the original consequences (a $25 million profit and a 21% market share). (See tables 11-3 and 11-4.)

TABLE 11-3

Charting the consequences

	ALTERNATIVES	
Objectives	Franchising	Not franchising
Profit (in millions of $)	10	25
Market share (%)	26	21

TABLE 11-4

Making the even swap

	ALTERNATIVES	
Objectives	Franchising	Not franchising
~~Profit (in millions of $)~~	~~10~~	~~25~~ 10
Market share (%)	26	~~21~~ 24

Fourth, cancel out the now-irrelevant objective

Now that the profits for the two alternatives are equivalent, profit can be eliminated as a consideration in the decision. It all boils down to market share.

Finally, select the dominant alternative

The new decision is easy. The franchising alternative, better on market share than not franchising, is the obvious choice.

For the cola company, only one even swap revealed the superior alternative. Usually, it takes more—often many more. The beauty of the even-swap approach is that no matter how many alternatives and objectives you're weighing, you can methodically reduce the number of objectives you need to consider until a clear choice emerges. The method, in other words, is iterative. You keep eliminating objectives by making additional even swaps until one alternative dominates all the others or until only one objective—one basis of comparison—remains.

John S. Hammond is a consultant on decision making and a former professor at Harvard Business School in Boston. **Ralph L. Keeney** is a professor at Duke University's Fuqua School of Business in Durham, North Carolina. **Howard Raiffa** is the Frank Plumpton Ramsey Professor of Managerial Economics (Emeritus) at Harvard Business School. They are the coauthors of *Smart Choices: A Practical Guide to Making Better Decisions* (Harvard Business Review Press, 2015).

CHAPTER 12

Making Better Decisions with Less Data

by Tanya Menon and Leigh Thompson

Maria, an executive in financial services, stared at another calendar invite that would surely kill three hours of her day. Whenever a tough problem presented itself, her boss's knee-jerk response was, "Collect more data!" Maria appreciated her boss's analytical approach, but as the surveys, reports, and stats began to pile up, it was clear that the team was stuck in analysis paralysis. And despite the many meetings, task forces, brainstorming sessions, and workshops created to solve any given issue,

Adapted from "How to Make Better Decisions with Less Data," on hbr.org, November 7, 2016 (product #H038UJ).

the team tended to offer the same solutions—often ones that were recycled from prior problems.

As part of our research for our book, *Stop Spending, Start Managing*, we asked 83 executives how much they estimated that their companies wasted on relentless analytics on a daily basis. They reported a whopping $7,731 per day—$2,822,117 per year! Yet despite all of the data available, people often struggle to convert it into effective solutions to problems. Instead, they fall prey to what James March and his coauthors describe as "garbage can" decision making: a process whereby actors, problems, and possible solutions swirl about in a metaphorical garbage can and people end up agreeing on whatever solution rises to the top.[1] The problem isn't *lack* of data inside the garbage can; the vast amount of data means managers struggle to prioritize what's important. In the end, they end up applying arbitrary data toward new problems, reaching a subpar solution.

To curb garbage-can decision making, managers and their teams should think more carefully about the information they need to solve a problem and think more strategically about how to apply it to their decision making and actions. We recommend the data DIET approach, which provides four steps of intentional thought to help convert data into knowledge and wisdom.

Step 1: Define

When teams and individuals think about a problem, they likely jump right into suggesting possible solutions. It's the basis of many brainstorming sessions. But while the prospect of problem solving sounds positive, people tend to fixate on familiar approaches rather than stepping back to understand the contours of the problem.

Start with a problem-finding mindset, where you loosen the definitions around the problem and allow people to see it from different angles, thereby exposing hidden assumptions and revealing new questions before the hunt for data begins.[2] With your team, think of critical questions about the problem in order to fully understand its complexity: How do you understand the problem? What are its causes? What assumptions does your team have? Alternately, write about the problem (without proposing solutions) from different perspectives—the customer, the supplier, and the competitor, for example—to see the situation in new ways.

Once you have a better view of the problem, you can move forward with a disciplined data search. Avoid decision-making delays by holding data requests accountable to if-then statements. Ask yourself a simple question: If I collect the data, then how would my decision change? If the data won't change your decision, you don't need to track down the additional information.

Step 2: Integrate

Once you've defined the problem and the data you need, you must use that information effectively. In the example above, Maria felt frustrated because as the team members collected more and more pieces of the jigsaw puzzle, they weren't investing the same amount of time to see how the pieces fit together. Their subconscious beliefs or assumptions about problems guided their behavior, causing them to follow the same tired routine time and time again: Collect data, hold meetings, create strategy moving forward. But this is garbage-can decision making. In order to keep the pieces from coming together in an arbitrary fashion, you need to look at the data differently.

Integration lets you analyze how your problem and data fit together, which then lets you break down your hidden assumptions. With your team, create a KJ diagram (named after author Kawakita Jiro and illustrated in figure 12-1) to sort facts into causal relationships. Write the facts on notecards and then sort them into piles based on observable relationships—for example, an increase in clients after a successful initiative, a drop in sales caused by a delayed project, or any other data points that may indicate correlated items or causal relationships. In doing this, you can create a visual model of the patterns that emerge and make connections in the data.

Step 3: Explore

At this point in the process, you may have some initial ideas or solutions based on your KJ diagrams. Now's the time to develop them. To facilitate collaborative exploration, one of our favorite exercises (often used in art schools) is what we call the passing game. Assign distinct ideas to each team member and give each individual five minutes to develop it by drawing or writing in silence. Then have them pass their work to a teammate, who continues drafting the idea while they take over a teammate's creation.

Discuss the collaborative output. Teammates recognize how it feels to give up "ownership" of an idea and

FIGURE 12-1

KJ diagram, in two steps

Step 1: Write facts on notecards.

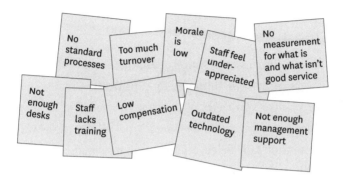

Step 2: Sort the notecards into piles based on observable relationships.

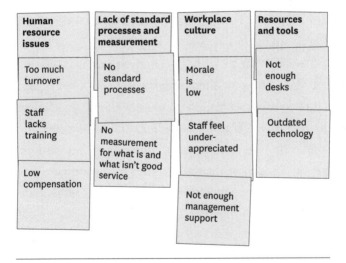

how it feels to both edit and be edited; they also recognize their implicit assumptions about collaboration. The new perspective forces them to confront directions that they didn't choose or never would have considered. Indeed, you can add multiple sequential passes (like a telephone game) to demonstrate the idea's unpredictable evolution as three or four teammates play with the initial ideas. After allowing people this space for exploration, discuss the directions that are most fruitful.

Step 4: Test

The last dimension requires team members to use their powers of critical thinking to consider feasibility and correct for overreach. Design tests to see if your plan forward will work. Under which types of situations will the solution fail? Select a few critical tests and run them. While people often overcollect data that supports their prior decisions, people undercollect disconfirming data. Running even a single test fights confirmation biases and allows you to see what you need to see, even if you don't want to.

The solution to garbage-can decisions isn't cutting out data entirely. Thinking strategically about your data needs pushes you to do more with less—widening, deepening, integrating, extending, and testing the data you do have to convert it into knowledge and wisdom. In practicing these mental exercises with your team, you can curb your appetite for data while getting better at digesting the data you have.

———————

Tanya Menon is an associate professor of management and human resources at the Ohio State University's Fisher College of Business. **Leigh Thompson** is a professor at the Kellogg School of Management at Northwestern University and the author of nine books, including

Creative Conspiracy: The New Rules of Breakthrough Collaboration (Harvard Business Review Press, 2013). They are the coauthors of *Stop Spending, Start Managing: Strategies to Transform Wasteful Habits* (Harvard Business Review Press, 2016).

NOTES

1. Michael D. Cohen, James G. March, and Johan P. Olsen, "A Garbage Can Model of Organizational Choice," *Administrative Science Quarterly* 17, no. 1 (1972): 1–25.

2. J. W. Getzels, "Problem Finding: A Theoretical Note," *Cognitive Science* 3, no. 2 (1979): 167–171.

CHAPTER 13

A Six-Part Tool for Ranking and Assessing Risks

by Luke Bencie and Sami Araboghli

One of the most overused expressions thrown around by wannabe "Wall Street Rambos" is *business is war*. But sometimes war tactics really can help in business.

Among these tactics is CARVER, a system for assessing and ranking threats and opportunities. Developed during World War II, CARVER (then one letter shorter and known as CARVE) was originally used by analysts to determine where bomber pilots could most effectively drop their munitions on enemy targets. It can be both

Adapted from content posted on hbr.org, September 21, 2018 (product #H04JV4).

offensive and defensive, meaning it can be used for identifying your competitors' weaknesses and for internal auditing. In addition, many security experts consider it the definitive assessment tool for protecting critical assets. In fact, the U.S. Department of Homeland Security has recommended it as a preferred assessment methodology. (One of us, Luke, is so enthusiastic about CARVER that he cowrote a book on it.)

More recently, CARVER has converted a new community of believers in the business world, including CEOs, financial analysts, and risk management planners, not to mention a number of *Fortune* 500 security directors. Since it draws on both qualitative and quantitative data, CARVER can be applied in almost any scenario that is analyzed and discussed in an organized, logical way. It can be highly useful if you need to, for example, defend a budget request or a strategic plan to company leadership. Because it helps you articulate an efficient story using numeric values, you can use CARVER to clarify mission objectives—whether on the battlefield or in the boardroom. You might say CARVER is a SWOT analysis on steroids.

CARVER is an acronym that stands for:

- **Criticality.** How essential an asset or critical system is to your company

- **Accessibility.** How hard it would be for an adversary to access or attack the asset

- **Recoverability.** How quickly you could recover if something happened to the asset

- **Vulnerability.** How well (or not) the asset could withstand an adversary's attack

- **Effect.** How much of an impact there would be across your business if something happened to the asset

- **Recognizability.** How likely it is that an adversary would recognize the asset as a valuable target

To use CARVER—whether you're assessing a system, a business goal, or something else—you assign scores from 1 to 5 (with 5 being "most essential," "most likely," and so on) for each of the six criteria. The sum of the six scores is the total score for whatever you're assessing. Once you've calculated the total scores for a few things, you can compare them. For example, you could use CARVER to compare two business opportunities; whichever has the higher score is probably the better option to pursue.

Here's an example. Let's say the chief security officer for an oil and gas company is deciding how to allocate the budget across multiple locations and assets. At a strategic level, the CSO could use CARVER to think through the factors involved for each location and then allocate resources for each facility.

To start, the CSO would ask a series of questions related to the CARVER criteria. Beginning with criticality, they might ask, "How critical is the oil pipeline in Abuja, Nigeria, to the company's overall operations?" Because criticality is based on the importance of the asset (in this case, the pipeline), the CSO would need to determine if the destruction or compromise of this asset would have a significant impact on the output, mission, or operation of the company. The CSO would rank criticality like this:

5—Loss of the pipeline would stop operations

4—Loss would reduce operations considerably

3—Loss would reduce operations

2—Loss may reduce operations

1—Loss would not affect operations

Obviously, the higher the number, the more detrimental the loss of the asset would be to the organization. The lower the number, the less detrimental the loss would be, or there might be redundancies in place—other pipelines, for example. (Those redundancies would also affect the asset's recoverability score.)

To assess the recoverability of that same pipeline (perhaps after a natural disaster, sabotage, or a terrorist attack), the CSO would rank it like this:

5—Extremely difficult to replace; long downtime

4—Difficult to replace; long downtime

3—Can be replaced in a relatively short time

2—Easily replaced in a short time

1—Can be replaced immediately; short or no downtime

The CSO would then continue ranking the Abuja pipeline on the other four criteria. If the pipeline received a 5 for criticality and recoverability, for example, it seems likely that it would be a good candidate to receive more of the CSO's budget.

To consider another example, say a hedge fund is looking to acquire a tech company that claims to have a leading-edge technology. In addition to simply auditing the company's books, analysts could perform a CARVER assessment to determine how close the competition might be to catching up to this technology, thus balancing the risk of the investment. The tech company may score low (meaning good) on criticality and recoverability but score high (meaning bad) on accessibility and effect. That accessibility score might mean a competitor could beat the product to market, and the effect could be the fallout from a controversial marketing campaign.

One question the analysts might ask for effect is: "What is the effect on us if the tech company's competitors beat us to market?"

5—Very high economic, political, or social impact on the organization

4—High economic, political, or social impact

3—Moderate impact

2—Little impact

1—No unfavorable impact

The important thing to remember is that this exercise is conducted to identify, categorize, and prioritize high-risk assets; to assess vulnerabilities; and to make recommendations around risk. Once a CARVER assessment has been completed and material risks and threats have been identified, security and risk management professionals can determine the best approach to take. Even the smallest difference in CARVER scores could influence whether you open a store in one location versus another, or help you decide between upgrading an existing product line and opting to create something new.

Strategic decisions are being made in boardrooms everywhere, by executives who are looking for any advantage over the competition. Business leaders are looking for hard numbers to provide them with an edge in their decision-making process. CARVER can provide a quantified justification for standing by—or abandoning—a decision or initiative.

Luke Bencie is the managing director of Security Management International. He has worked in over 100 countries for the Department of Defense, the U.S. intelligence community, and over two dozen *Fortune* 500 companies. He is author of *The CARVER Target Analysis and Vulnerability Assessment Methodology*, as well as *Among Enemies: Counter-Espionage for the Business Traveler*. **Sami Araboghli** is a junior associate at Security Management International. He is also a U.S. Marine Corp Reservist.

CHAPTER 14

How to Tackle Your Toughest Decisions

by Joseph L. Badaracco

Every manager makes tough calls—it comes with the
job. And the toughest calls come in the gray areas—situations where you and your team have worked hard to
gather the facts and done the best analysis you can, but
you still don't know what to do. It's easy to become paralyzed in the face of such challenges. Yet as a leader, you
have to make a decision and move forward. Your judgment becomes critical.

Judgment is hard to define. It is a fusion of your
thinking, feelings, experience, imagination, and char-
acter. But five practical questions can improve your odds

Reprinted from *Harvard Business Review*, September 2016 (product
#R1609J).

of making sound judgments, even when the data is incomplete or unclear, opinions are divided, and the answers are far from obvious.

Where do these questions come from? Over many centuries and across many cultures, they have emerged as men and women with serious responsibilities have struggled with difficult problems. They express the insights of the most penetrating minds and compassionate spirits of human history. I have relied on them for years, in teaching MBA candidates and counseling executives, and I believe that they can help you, your team, and your organization navigate the grayest of gray areas.

This article explains the five questions and illustrates them with a disguised case study involving a manager who must decide what to do about a persistently under-performing employee who has failed to respond to suggestions for improvement. He deserves a bad review, if not dismissal, but higher-ups at the company want to overlook his failings.

How should the manager approach this situation? Not by following her gut instinct. Not by simply falling into line. Instead, she needs to systematically work through the five questions:

What are the net, net consequences of all my options?

What are my core obligations?

What will work in the world as it is?

Who are we?

What can I live with?

To grapple with these questions, you must rely on the best information and expertise available. But in the end you have to answer them for yourself. With gray-area decisions, you can never be certain you've made the right call. But if you follow this process, you'll know that you worked on the problem in the right way—not just as a good manager but as a thoughtful human being.

Net, Net Consequences

The first question asks you to thoroughly and analytically consider every course of action available to you, along with the full, real-world, human consequences of each. Gray-area problems are rarely resolved in a flash of intuitive brilliance from one person; as a very successful CEO told me, "The lonely leader on Olympus is really a bad model." So your job is to put aside your initial assumption about what you *should* do, gather a group of trusted advisers and experts, and ask yourself and them, "What *could* we do? And who will be hurt or helped, short-term and long-term, by each option?"

Don't confuse this with cost-benefit analysis, or focus solely on what you can count or price. Of course, you should get the best data you can and apply the relevant frameworks. But gray-area problems require you to think more broadly, deeply, concretely, imaginatively, and objectively about the full impact of your choices. In the words of the ancient Chinese philosopher Mozi, "It is the business of the benevolent man to seek to promote what is beneficial to the world and to eliminate what is harmful."

In today's complex, fluid, interdependent world, none of us can predict the future with total accuracy. And it's sometimes hard to think clearly about gray-area issues. What's important is taking the time to open your mind, assemble the right team, and analyze your options through a humanist lens. You might sketch out a rough decision tree, listing all potential moves and all probable outcomes, or designate certain people to act as devil's advocates to find holes in your thinking and prevent you from rushing to conclusions or succumbing to groupthink.

When you make important, difficult decisions, you affect many people's lives and livelihoods. The first question asks you to grapple hard with that reality.

Core Obligations

We all have duties—as parents, children, citizens, employees. Managers also have duties to shareholders and other stakeholders. But the second question gets at something deeper: the duties we have to safeguard and respect the lives, rights, and dignity of our fellow men and women.

All the world's great religions—Islam, Judaism, Hinduism, Christianity—emphasize this obligation. The contemporary ethicist Kwame Anthony Appiah has said, "No local loyalty can ever justify forgetting that each human being has responsibilities to every other."

How can you figure out specifically what these duties oblige you to do in a particular situation? By relying on what philosophers call your "moral imagination." That involves stepping out of your comfort zone, recognizing your biases and blind spots, and putting yourself in the shoes of all key stakeholders, especially the most vulnerable ones. How would you feel in their place? What would you be most concerned about or afraid of? How would you want to be treated? What would you see as fair? What rights would you believe you had? What would you consider to be hateful? You might speak directly to the people who will be affected by your decision, or ask a member of your team to role-play the outsider or victim as persuasively as he or she can.

Again, you must look past economics and your business school training. Yes, managers have a legal duty to serve the corporation—but that's a very broad mandate that includes the well-being of workers, customers, and the community in which they operate. You have serious obligations to everyone simply because you are a human being. When you face a gray-area decision, you have to think—long, hard, and personally—about which of these duties stands at the head of the line.

The World as It Is

The third question pushes you to look at your problem in a clear-eyed, pragmatic way—seeing the world not as you would like it to be but as it is. Ultimately you need a plan that will work—one that will move an individual, a team, a department, or an entire organization through a gray area responsibly and successfully.

The phrase "the world as it is" points toward Niccolò Machiavelli's thinking—a perspective that might seem surprising in an article about making responsible decisions. But his view is important, because it acknowledges that we don't live in a predictable, calm environment populated with virtuous people. The world Machiavelli described is unpredictable, difficult, and shaped by self-interest. Sound plans can turn out badly, and bad plans sometimes work. Much of what happens is simply beyond our control. Leaders rarely have unlimited freedom and resources, so they must often make painful choices. And a great many individuals and groups will pursue their own agendas, skillfully or clumsily, if not persuaded to do otherwise.

That is why, after considering consequences and duties, you need to think about practicalities: Of the possible solutions to your problem, which is most likely to work? Which is most resilient? And how resilient and flexible are you?

To answer those questions, you need to map the force field of power around you: who wants what and how hard and successfully each person can fight for his aims. You must also ready yourself to be agile and even opportunistic—maneuvering around any roadblocks or surprises—and, when the situation calls for it, to play hardball, asserting your authority and reminding others who is the boss.

It's easy to misinterpret the third question as an "out"—an excuse to do what's safe and expedient instead of the right thing. But the question is really about what will work if you bring persistence, dedication, creativity, prudent risk-taking, and political savvy to the task.

Who Are We?

According to an old African adage, "I am because we are." Put differently, our behavior and identities are shaped by the groups in which we work and live. As Aristotle said (and as a vast body of scientific literature has since confirmed), "Man is by nature a social animal." So this question asks you to step back and think about your decision in terms of relationships, values, and norms. What really matters to your team, company, community, culture? How can you act in a way that reflects and expresses those belief systems? If they conflict, which should take precedence?

To answer those questions, you might think about the defining stories of a particular group—the decisions and incidents that everyone cites when explaining the ideals to which you are collectively committed, what you have struggled to achieve, and what outcomes you try hard to avoid. Imagine that you are writing a sentence or a chapter in your company's history. Of all the paths you might choose in this gray area, which would best express what your organization stands for?

This question comes fourth because you shouldn't start with it. Unlike the first three, which require you to take an outsider's perspective on your situation and consider it as objectively as possible, this one addresses you as an insider, at risk for adopting an insular, limited view when you consider norms and values, because we are naturally inclined to take care of our own. So counterbalance that tendency with the thinking prompted by the previous questions.

Living with Your Decision

Good judgment relies on two things: One is the best possible understanding and analysis of the situation. The other involves the values, ideals, vulnerabilities, and experiences of whoever will be making the decision. A seasoned executive once told me, "I wouldn't go ahead with something just because my brain told me it was the right thing to do. I also had to feel it. If I didn't, I had to get my brain and my gut into harmony."

Ultimately you must choose, commit to, act on, and live with the consequences of your choice. So it must also reflect what you really care about as a manager and a human being. After considering outcomes, duties, practicalities, and values, you must decide what matters most and what matters less. This has always been the challenge of taking on any serious responsibilities at work and in life.

How will you figure out what you can live with? End your conversations with others, close the door, mute the electronics, and stop to reflect. Imagine yourself explaining your decision to a close friend or a mentor—someone you trust and respect deeply. Would you feel comfortable? How would that person react? It may also be helpful to write down your decision and your reasons for it: Writing forces clearer thinking and serves as a form of personal commitment.

In Practice

Now let's turn to our case study. Becky Friedman was the 27-year-old manager of a 14-person technology group responsible for clothing sales at an online retailer. One of her team members, Terry Fletcher, a man 15 years her senior with a longer tenure at the company, wasn't doing his part. Although his previous boss had routinely given him scores of 3.5 on their five-point performance scale, Friedman didn't believe his work merited that; and whenever she presented him with opportunities to develop his skills and ramp up his contributions, he failed to follow through. So she wanted to drop his rating to 2.5 and put him on a performance improvement plan (PIP), on a path to dismissal. Soon, however, two of the company's vice presidents, good friends of Fletcher's, caught wind of her plans and paid her a visit. They asked whether she was sure about what she was doing and suggested that the real problem might be her management.

Suddenly the situation was no longer black-and-white. Friedman had entered a gray area and felt stuck. To find a way out, she turned to the five questions. She considered her options—stick to her plan, abandon it, or find a middle ground—and their consequences. She reminded herself of her basic duties to her fellow human beings, including Fletcher, her team, and the VPs. She evaluated the practical realities of her organization. She weighed the defining norms and values of her various social groups. And she thought carefully about her own abiding sense of what really matters in life.

She suspected that if she pushed forward and gave Fletcher the rating he deserved, she and her team would suffer retribution: The VPs could withhold resources or even force her out of the company. She also worried about Fletcher, who seemed off-balance and appeared to have few things going well in his life. How would a poor review and a possible job loss affect him, not just financially but also psychologically? If Friedman chose option B, however, she would still have a deadweight on her team, which might prevent the group from achieving its ambitious goals and demoralize its most talented and diligent members. The VPs might also take her capitulation as a sign of weakness, which could keep her, a relative newcomer, from moving up in the leadership ranks.

Middle-ground options, such as presenting Fletcher with further development opportunities or giving him another warning, seemed more promising but carried their own risks: Would they be effective in changing his behavior? Would they still result in backlash from the VPs? Friedman also thought about what she, her team, and her organization cared about most. As a woman in computer science, she knew what it was like to be marginalized, as Fletcher was among the whiz kids in her department, and she felt compelled to help him. At the same time, her group prided itself on exceptionally professional performance, and her company, although young, had always claimed and generally proved to be a meritocracy with high standards and a sharp focus on customer needs.

After much deliberation, Friedman decided to try a counseling session with Fletcher. She opened by telling him that she had decided to give him a 2.5, but that she wouldn't put him on a PIP because it would be too demeaning. She then asked him to consider the department's recent hires—all of whom had strong technical skills—and honestly evaluate whether he would be happy or successful working alongside them. She concluded by suggesting that he spend the next several months continuing to do his job while also looking for another one. She was surprised and relieved when his immediate anger over the bad rating subsided and he agreed to consider her plan; in fact, he had already been toying with the idea of leaving. He spent the next several weeks looking for other positions, inside the company and elsewhere, and soon joined another company. Friedman, meanwhile, continued to thrive. She had, of course, been lucky; there was no guarantee that Fletcher would respond so positively to her feedback. But she'd put herself in a good position by getting the process right, and she'd been prepared to try other, equally thought-through tactics if the first didn't work.

When you face a gray-area problem, be sure to systematically answer *all five* of the questions, just as Becky Friedman did. Don't simply pick your favorite. Each question is an important voice in the centuries-long conversation about what counts as a sound decision regarding a hard problem with high stakes for other people.

Leadership can be a heavy burden. It is also a compelling, crucial challenge. In gray areas, your job isn't *finding* solutions; it's *creating* them, relying on your judgment. As an executive I greatly respect once told me, "We really want someone or some rule to tell us what to do. But sometimes there isn't one, and *you* have to decide what the most relevant rules or principles are in this particular case. You can't escape that responsibility."

Joseph L. Badaracco is the John Shad Professor of Business Ethics at Harvard Business School, where he has taught courses on leadership, strategy, corporate responsibility, and management. His books on these subjects include *New York Times* bestseller *Leading Quietly*, *Defining Moments*, and *Managing in the Gray*. His latest book, *Step Back: How to Bring the Art of Reflection into Your Busy Life*, will be published by Harvard Business Review Press in 2020.

CHAPTER 15

When It's Safe to Rely on Intuition (and When It's Not)

by Connson Chou Locke

We often use mental shortcuts, or heuristics, to make decisions. There is simply too much information coming at us from all directions, and too many decisions that we need to make from moment to moment, to think every single one through a long and detailed analysis. While this can sometimes backfire, in many cases intuition is a perfectly fine shortcut. However, intuition is helpful only under certain conditions.

Adapted from content posted on hbr.org, April 30, 2015 (product #H021HY).

The most important condition is *expertise.* If I am a novice mountain climber, then my intuition on whether or not a given route is safe is not going to be accurate—I have no previous knowledge on which to base that decision. Similarly, if a financial history professor is making an investment decision, her expertise in financial history does not automatically extend to financial investments; thus she should not rely on intuition for those decisions.

It takes a surprising amount of domain-specific expertise to develop accurate intuitive judgments—around 10 years, according to the research. And during this time, repetition and feedback are essential. For example, a TV show producer, in order to develop accurate intuitive judgment about new television shows, would need to repeatedly engage in making decisions about new shows and receive rapid and accurate feedback on whether those choices were good ones. Eventually, this repetition and feedback become embedded as intuitive learning and can be used to make fast and effective intuitive decisions about new shows.

Learning can also happen subconsciously over time (also called "implicit learning"). For example, a factory foreman spends every day scanning the factory environment, ensuring it is safe and workers are productive. After many years of this, the foreman learns to recognize the most important signals or patterns of activity, ignoring irrelevant information. Thus, the experienced foreman can respond to conditions on the factory floor in a rapid, accurate, and intuitive way.

The second condition relates to the type of decision you're making. To be conducive to intuitive judgment, the problem should be *unstructured*. An unstructured problem is one that lacks clear decision rules or has few objective criteria with which to make the decision—for example, aesthetic judgments about whether a new movie or art exhibit will be a success, political judgments regarding the best way to get a new initiative approved, or human resource judgments concerning the best way to resolve a conflict between employees.

The types of problems that do *not* benefit from intuition are ones that have clear decision rules, objective criteria, and abundant data with which to perform an analysis. In making a medical diagnosis, for example, computer algorithms tend to be more accurate than an experienced medical doctor's judgment. This is because the computer can calculate the probability that a certain set of symptoms indicate a particular illness while also factoring in the patient's age, sex, and other relevant factors. The human brain, when faced with such a large amount of data, must use heuristics, and those mental shortcuts can be imperfect. With hundreds of possible symptoms and illnesses, it would be very difficult for any individual doctor to develop the depth of expertise required to make an accurate intuitive judgment on a specific illness.

Of course, most decisions lie somewhere between the aesthetic judgment and computer algorithm. In buying a new car, you can feed data into a computer algorithm to calculate the most efficient and economical model for your needs, but the final decision will be influenced by your reaction to the look and feel of the car—something a computer cannot assess for you. Likewise, the decision to sell your product in a new market can be analyzed quantitatively, but the final outcome will be affected by the new customers' feelings about the product—something a computer cannot predict. Nonetheless, if there are clear decision rules that can be used to create an algorithm, if relevant data are available, and if the decision will be assessed with purely objective criteria (that is, not aesthetic judgments or feelings), then an analytical approach is likely to be more helpful than intuition in reaching the best decision.

Finally, the third condition is the amount of *time* you have available. If you only have a small window in which to decide, intuition can be helpful because it is faster than a detailed analysis. This is especially true when there is very little information with which to make the decision. When information and time are scarce, using heuristics such as intuition can often be as effective as a rational approach. However, lack of time by itself is not necessarily a good reason to use intuition. As much as we want to believe that our intuition is telling us something meaningful, it is still a shortcut that could lead us down the wrong path.

Intuition is essentially a feeling, and we do not know the source of that feeling. It may be that our aversion to a particular option is reflecting a hidden nervousness, insecurity, or fear of the unknown. If so, then our intuition will lead us to reject a perfectly good option. At the same time, research has found that feelings are relevant—even essential—to decision making; a study of patients with a tumor in the emotion area of the brain found they could generate alternatives but were unable to choose one.

Ultimately, it may be that we should use both intuition and analysis. There may be times when intuition helps narrow down the options, which can then be evaluated in a logical and rational way. Or the reverse: An initial detailed analysis may identify a few options that seem equally good, and intuition is needed to single out the right one. But before you decide to trust your gut, ask yourself: Am I an expert? Is this an unstructured problem? And how much time do I have to choose?

Connson Chou Locke, PhD, is a leadership researcher, teacher, consultant, and coach, specializing in leadership development, culture, and change. She is Senior Lecturer in Practice at the London School of Economics and Political Science. Locke is available for speaking and workshops. Follow her on LinkedIn and Twitter @connsonlocke.

Make the Choice and Follow Through

CHAPTER 16

Stop Worrying About Making the Right Decision

by Ed Batista

Much of my work as a coach involves helping people wrestle with an important decision. Some of these choices feel particularly big because they involve selecting one option to the exclusion of all others when the cost of being "wrong" can be substantial: *If I'm at a crossroads in my career, which path should I follow? If I'm considering job offers, which one should I accept? If I'm being asked to relocate, should I move to a new city or stay put?*

Difficult decisions like these remind me of a comment made by Scott McNealy—a cofounder and former

---

Adapted from content posted on hbr.org, November 8, 2013.

CEO of Sun Microsystems—during a lecture I attended while I was in business school at Stanford: He was asked how he made decisions and responded by saying, in effect, "It's important to make good decisions. But I spend much less time and energy worrying about 'making the right decision' and much more time and energy ensuring that any decision I make turns out right."

I'm paraphrasing, but my memory of this comment is vivid, and his point was crystal clear. Before we make any decision—particularly one that will be difficult to undo—we're understandably anxious and focused on identifying the "best" option because of the risk of being "wrong." (See the sidebar "How Anxiety Can Lead Your Decisions Astray.") But a by-product of that mindset is that we overemphasize the moment of choice and lose sight of everything that follows. Merely selecting the "best" option doesn't guarantee that things will turn out well in the long run, just as making a suboptimal choice doesn't doom us to failure or unhappiness. It's what happens next (and in the days, months, and years that follow) that ultimately determines whether a given decision was "right."

Another aspect of this dynamic is that our focus on making the right decision can easily lead to paralysis, because the options we're choosing among are so difficult to rank in the first place. How can we definitively determine in advance what career path will be best, what job offer to accept, or whether to move across the country or stay put? Obviously, we can't. There are far too many variables. But the more we yearn for an objective algorithm to rank our options and make the decision for us,

HOW ANXIETY CAN LEAD YOUR DECISIONS ASTRAY

by Francesca Gino

My colleagues and I undertook research to understand how anxiety impacts people's willingness to accept advice from others and their likelihood of following poor guidance. The upshot? Our natural instincts can get us into a lot of trouble.

In one of our studies, we asked college students to look at a photo of a stranger and estimate that person's weight. We told them that they would receive a $1 bonus per photo if they came within 10 pounds of the right answer. After completing the initial task, some participants were shown an anxiety-inducing clip from the movie *Vertical Limit*; the rest watched a "neutral" clip from a *National Geographic* documentary about fish in the Great Barrier Reef. Next, students rated their self-confidence and then completed another round of weight estimates. But before being shown the photographs again, the students indicated whether they wanted to receive advice from someone else before making their guesses. Those put in an anxious state by the movie clip felt less confident than those who watched the nature documentary. Ninety percent of those in the anxiety condition opted to seek advice; only 72% of those in the neutral state did. Those in the anxious state were also more likely to take the advice they were given.

(continued)

HOW ANXIETY CAN LEAD YOUR DECISIONS ASTRAY

This might not be a problem, except that anxiety also impairs our ability to accurately judge the quality of the advice we receive. In a follow-up to this experiment, my colleagues and I had another group of participants write about an experience from the past that made them anxious or about their last visit to the grocery store (typically a neutral experience) and then estimate the number of coins in a jar. This time, some participants were given bad advice; others were given good advice (that is, they received accurate estimates of the number of coins). Those who were in a neutral state were more likely to take advice when it was good rather than bad. But anxious participants tended to make no such distinction. Anxiety reduced their ability to discern between good and bad advice.

These two tendencies—being more receptive to advice and less discriminating—can combine in a way that can be harmful. In fact, in a similar study, we found that people who were made to feel anxious were

the more we distance ourselves from the subjective factors—our intuition, our emotions, our gut—that will ultimately pull us in one direction or another. So we get stuck, waiting for a sign to point the way.

I believe the path to getting unstuck when faced with a daunting, possibly paralyzing decision is embedded in McNealy's comment, and it involves a fundamental re-more open to, and more likely to rely on, advice even when they knew that the person offering it had a conflict of interest—that is, when he or she would benefit financially from the participant taking the advice.

The anxiety we triggered in our experiments was relatively mild. By contrast, the anxiety prompted by high-stake decisions can be so great that it can overwhelm our careful plans and analysis.

———————

Francesca Gino is a behavioral scientist and the Tandon Family Professor of Business Administration at Harvard Business School. She is the author of the books *Rebel Talent: Why It Pays to Break the Rules at Work and in Life* and *Sidetracked: Why Our Decisions Get Derailed, and How We Can Stick to the Plan*. Follow her on Twitter @francescagino.

Adapted from content posted on hbr.org, October 29, 2013 (product #H00H49).

orientation of our mindset: Focusing on the choice minimizes the effort that will inevitably be required to make any option succeed and diminishes our sense of agency and ownership. In contrast, focusing on the effort that will be required *after* our decision not only helps us see the means by which any choice might succeed, but also restores our sense of agency and reminds us that while randomness plays a role in every outcome, our locus of control resides in our day-to-day activities more than in our onetime decisions.

So while I support using available data to rank options in some rough sense, ultimately we're best served by avoiding paralysis-by-analysis and moving forward by:

1. Paying close attention to the feelings and emotions that accompany the decision we're facing

2. Assessing how motivated we are to work toward the success of any given option

3. Recognizing that no matter what option we choose, our efforts to support its success will be more important than the initial guesswork that led to our choice

This view is consistent with the work of Stanford professor Baba Shiv, an expert in the neuroscience of decision making. Shiv notes that in the case of complex decisions, rational analysis will get us closer to a decision but won't result in a definitive choice because our options involve trading one set of appealing outcomes for another, and the complexity of each scenario makes it impossible to determine in advance which outcome will be optimal.

Two key findings have emerged from Shiv's research: First, successful decisions are those in which the decision maker remains committed to their choice. And second, emotions play a critical role in determining a successful outcome to a trade-off decision. As Shiv told *Stanford Business Magazine*, emotions are "mental shortcuts that help us resolve trade-off conflicts and . . . happily commit to a decision." Going further, Shiv noted, "When you feel a trade-off conflict, it just behooves you to focus on your gut."

This isn't to say that we should simply allow our emotions to choose for us. We've all made "emotional" decisions that we later came to regret. But current neuroscience research makes clear that emotions are an important input into decision making by ruling out the options most likely to lead to a negative outcome and focusing our attention on the options likely to lead to a positive outcome. More specifically, research by Florida State professor Roy Baumeister and others suggests that good decision making is tied to our ability to anticipate *future* emotional states. As they note in their book *Do Emotions Help or Hurt Decisionmaking?*, "It is not what a person feels right now, but what he or she anticipates feeling as the result of a particular behavior that can be a powerful and effective guide to choosing well."

When we're stuck or even paralyzed by a decision, we need more than rational analysis. We need to vividly envision ourselves in a future scenario, get in touch with the emotions this generates, and assess how those feelings influence our level of commitment to that particular choice. We can't always make the right decision, but we can make every decision right.

———

Ed Batista is an executive coach and lecturer at the Stanford Graduate School of Business. He writes regularly on issues related to coaching and professional development at edbatista.com, contributed to the *HBR Guide to Coaching Your Employees* (Harvard Business Review Press, 2015), and is currently writing a book on self-coaching for Harvard Business Review Press. Follow him on Twitter @edbatista.

CHAPTER 17

When to Stop Deliberating and Just Make the Call

by Thomas H. Davenport

You've come up with ideas, narrowed down your options, and looked at the available data. You've asked all the right questions to guide your choice. And yet, for some reason, you just can't pull the trigger on a decision. What's the holdup?

Whether you've experienced this indecision yourself or you've known a leader or executive with the habit, it can be incredibly problematic—and potentially damaging—to sit on decisions. Waiting too long to decide can

---

Adapted from "When to Stop Deliberating and Just Make a Decision," on hbr.org, July 9, 2 019 (product #H051AJ).

slow businesses down, frustrate employees, and mean missing critical opportunities. When should you just make a choice versus gathering more data or cogitating on it longer?

In order to figure out whether a decision requires further time or should just be made, you need to do a little "meta-decision analysis" or, put simply, decide how to decide. Of course, that can extend the time for making a decision, but perhaps not by much. In order to decide when you need to make your choice, you have to think about its importance and its urgency, and whether you can use some organizational decision-making approaches to make it more accurate and likely to be correct.

Consider the Importance of Your Decision

The single most critical factor in determining how long a decision should take is how important it is. Choices of little consequence should not take very long. So the first step in deciding how to decide should be to ask yourself—or others, if you don't trust your own judgment—how much difference the decision makes. If it won't make a big difference to your life or business, just make the call and move on. Then you can devote your scarce time and brainpower to the decisions that really matter.

For more important choices, there are two good reasons for extending your decision-making process a bit. One is to reflect, and the other is to gather data and analyze it. Reflection—particularly when you can engage the unconscious mind—can be a good way to determine which factors are most important in a complex decision. Some observers recommend sleeping on a decision after reviewing the key factors around it, but there are other ways to engage the unconscious mind as well. Rest, play, meditation, or even taking a shower may do the trick. In any case, reflecting on a decision won't require much additional time; a day or night should be sufficient.

The other good reason for waiting to decide is to gather data and analyze it. Evidence across many decision domains has shown that data- and analytics-based decisions are more accurate than those made by human intuition. However, gathering data takes a lot of time— and analysis can take a while, too. But if it's an important decision and the data exists somewhere, a data-driven approach is probably worth the effort, particularly if you're going to make the decision multiple times.

Determine How Often the Same Decision Will Be Made

Whether and how often a decision is repeated is an important factor in the speed of decision making. If the decision is one that you make often—for example, pricing, inventory reordering, or hiring decisions—it may be worth investing in an analytical approach. Decisions that you repeat regularly are also likely to generate data; capturing the inputs and the outcomes of the choice makes it possible to produce a model that optimizes positive results. The first time a repetitive decision is treated analytically, it will be time consuming to gather and analyze the data to create a model. But it's worth taking this extra time up front, since every instance of the decision thereafter can be made much faster and with a high degree of accuracy.

Decisions that are both important and rare are often quite strategic, such as, "Should we change our business model?" or "Should we acquire our biggest competitor?" It may be possible to acquire some information related to these types of decisions, but probably not enough to create an analytical model. Such decisions are worth spending time on, but after you've viewed them from a variety of perspectives, they're not likely to get better with time. Waiting too long to settle on an answer may mean that the opportunity passes you by.

Look into Buying an Option

If a strategic decision involves a lot of uncertainty and you can't make it after some deliberation, one approach to easing the process is to buy an option from which you will learn more.

Options are well known in investing, where buying an option gives the investor the right to buy an asset at a particular price in the future. In decision making, it means taking a small step to learn more, before making a call that could significantly impact your people or the organization. For example, instead of acquiring a company, buying an option might mean creating a partnership or investing a smaller amount in the company than the cost required for a purchase. Buying an option as a decision-making approach can both ease and speed up the process for important decisions, and can result in a better eventual outcome if you take advantage of the learning opportunities the option provides. Keep in mind, of course, that buying an option shouldn't be an excuse for avoiding or delaying substantial action that your organization needs to take.

Put a Clock on Your Decision

Finally, if you find yourself struggling to make a choice, give it a deadline. You can quickly assess this timeline when you are first facing the decision or after you've deliberated. As one of the most important components of your meta-decision analysis, the due date will guide many other aspects of your approach. It determines, for example, whether you can employ data and analytics, whether you should involve more people, whether you can study the issues thoroughly, and even whether you can sleep on the decision overnight.

Several ways to improve the timing of decisions that I've mentioned suggest an organizational process for decision making, rather than relying on individual approaches and whims for every choice. While an organization can get carried away with decision bureaucracy, in general it's wise to not leave important decisions totally up to individuals—even the CEO. Good decision making only happens through the use of effective methods, ex post facto analysis, and reflection about how to improve. Putting a clock on decisions and monitoring how long they take are also actions that organizations are likely to be better at than individuals.

Yes, it's important sometimes to just make a choice, but not at the expense of systematic thought about how best to go about it. By taking these steps and strategically deciding how to decide, you'll find that you can break out of indecision and finally move forward.

Thomas H. Davenport is the President's Distinguished Professor in Management and Information Technology at Babson College, a research fellow at the MIT Initiative on the Digital Economy, and a senior adviser at Deloitte Analytics. He is the author of over a dozen management books, including *Only Humans Need Apply: Winners and Losers in the Age of Smart Machines* and *The AI Advantage.*

CHAPTER 18

What to Do After You Choose

A decision—especially an important one—is a milestone and not the end of the road. After a choice is made, you need to turn it into action. The way you communicate the decision to others will to some degree determine your success. Explain the thinking behind your decision and notify everyone who may be affected by your choice.

Explain the Decision

Always describe the thinking behind a final decision. It's important to be clear about why that alternative was chosen, as opposed to others. Explaining builds trust in the leadership's intentions and confidence that the choice was made for the benefit of the entire company.

Adapted from *Harvard Business Essentials: Decision Making* (product #7618), Harvard Business School Press, 2006.

Understanding the process, too, will help your people recognize how their own contributions were taken into account. For instance, if, during the decision-making process, team members were encouraged to question and debate each other's ideas, they are more likely to believe that their own viewpoints were given serious consideration. Even if the participants' viewpoints did not prevail, knowing that they were taken seriously will lend credibility to the process and acceptance of the final decision.

Notify the Right People

Ensure that everyone affected by the decision understands the decision and its consequences. New responsibilities need to be spelled out, as do performance expectations and penalties for failure. When people clearly understand expectations, they can focus on what needs to be done.

Notify everyone who is responsible for implementing the decision as well as anyone affected by it. Your list might also include the key stakeholders: members of your unit who were not part of the decision-making group, as well as senior management, department supervisors, external constituents, and even customers if they will see a change in the way you do business with them.

Your message to these individuals should include the following:

- **A statement of the issue that was addressed.**
  "Our bonus policy hasn't effectively differentiated between high and low performers. The bonus

checks of our top-quartile performers are not much higher than those of the bottom quartile."

- **A description of the objectives or decision-making criteria.** "We set out with a clear objective: to restructure the bonus system to reward people relative to their contributions."

- **The names and roles of the people involved in making the decision and why they were included.** "Our decision team included people with special insights into the issue: Sharon Henderson, director of benefits and compensation; Stan Halloway, our COO . . ."

- **The alternatives considered (and possibly a summary of the analysis in table form).** "After a period of benchmarking best-practice companies, we zeroed in on the three options shown in this chart . . ."

- **An explanation of the final decision and what it means for the key stakeholders.** "In the end, we found option B to be the best choice, given our objective of scaling bonuses to measurable contributions. Sharon will explain how it's structured and what it means for you."

- **The implementation plan and time frame.** "Everyone who is eligible for the bonus plan will receive a brochure explaining how it works and how it's tied to our system of performance reviews. It will go into effect at the beginning of the next quarter."

- **Recognition of those who participated.** "This new plan reflects the ideas and the hard work of many people. Every employee owes them thanks for their contributions."

- **Solicitation of feedback.** "One of the things we learned is that no bonus system is perfect. This one may not be perfect either. And as we roll out this new process, we'll know more about where it can be improved. We encourage all of you to give us feedback, since you are those most affected by this decision. As you see ways to better achieve our objective of rewarding performance, tell me, tell Sharon, tell your boss. Your ideas matter in this company."

Take the time to create a clear, concise message. An incomplete or poorly articulated message about the decision can lead to confusion, disappointment, and unwillingness to support execution.

After a final choice has been made and communicated, some members of the team will have to give up their preferred solutions. If they perceive the decision-making process as fair, this shouldn't be a problem. There's plenty of evidence that perceived fairness goes a long way in defusing opposition, creating legitimacy, and paving the way for support.

Be Transparent About Your Decision-Making Process

by Liane Davey

At some point in your career, you likely encountered a manager you believed was unfair. You probably thought to yourself, *When I'm a manager, I'm never going to be like that!* Now that you're in a management position yourself, you're probably dedicating significant amounts of time and energy to making unbiased decisions, but no doubt finding that the right balance is elusive. Sadly,

---

Adapted from "How to Earn a Reputation as a Fair Manager," on hbr.org, August 3, 2018 (product #H04H3P).

there is no objective measure of fairness. Instead, each time you attempt to level the playing field on one dimension, you throw it off balance on another. The best, if imperfect, approach is to understand the different forms of fairness and to be thoughtful about when and how you apply them.

You can start with the most standard measure of fairness, which focuses on the *outcomes* of your decisions. Did your decision-making process lead to a fair distribution (of inputs and outputs) for everyone involved? You can apply this test to common managerial decisions such as how you allocate workload, offer development opportunities, and dole out rewards and recognition. You can be sure that your team is scrutinizing the outcomes of these high-profile decisions. If one person is disadvantaged by your choices—for instance, assigned a less desirable shift or given a more difficult assignment— multiple times, it's likely that they will perceive your decision making as unfair.

If that was all you had to worry about, life would be relatively simple. Unfortunately, there's more to it. In addition to the fairness of the outcome, your team will be judging the fairness of your *process*. Was your decision-making process inherently fair, regardless of the outcome? For example, if you were evaluating performance, did you include the right factors, such as measuring salespeople on both the total revenue and the sale of the products or services that offer the most value to the organization? Was your assessment of the variables in your decision objective and unbiased? For instance, did you get input from multiple sources to reduce the likelihood of favoritism? How you arrive at your choice will carry as much weight in how you are perceived as the decision you ultimately end up making.

The challenge is that when you try to optimize one version of fairness, you can inadvertently taint the other. As a simple example, imagine assigning workloads based on a flip of a coin. Because a coin flip is random, it can be considered a fair *process*. Now imagine that you flip the coin 10 times and 7 of those times it comes up heads. The person who chose heads gets 70% of the workload— an unfair *outcome*. The takeaway is that you need to be mindful about both your decision-making process and the resulting outcomes. You might need to compromise on one form of fairness to avoid damaging the other.

One interesting side note: Research has suggested that the relative importance of the fairness of the outcome versus the fairness of the process depends on which an employee hears about *first*.[1] The research looked at a hypothetical hiring process in which some applicants were evaluated with a fair process and some with an unfair process: The difference was whether the evaluators scored all nine parts of the assessment protocol or only one of the nine. Some of the participants were told about the process that was used to make the selection decision before hearing whether or not they got the job, whereas others were told about the process after.

For those who heard about the process before the outcome, the fairness of the process—rather than whether they got the job or not—predicted their overall satisfaction. People who first heard about the process of evaluation, and later found out that they were ultimately not hired, were OK with that outcome because they believed the process leading to that decision had been fair. But for those who learned about the outcome first, the fairness of the outcome was more important. For example, when people first heard that they were not hired without any explanation of the process used to arrive at that decision, they immediately assumed that the decision was unfair. The study provides an important lesson: When you're using a fair process that might lead to an unfair allocation, be sure to provide details about the process before your team learns of the decision.

To this point, we have been talking about fairness as if it has a single definition that can be applied to either the process or the outcome of decision making. That, too, oversimplifies your challenge as a manager. There are two competing definitions of fairness—equality versus equity. In an egalitarian form of fairness, propriety is tied to how *equal* things are, whether that's having the same process or the same outcome for everyone. Vacation policies where everyone gets the same number of days off would be one example. In contrast, an equitable definition of fairness allows for either the process or the outcome to vary based on some legitimate and *equitable* difference among people. In the vacation example, you might give more time off to employees who have a longer tenure with the company. You end up with four different versions of fairness using either an equal or an equitable definition applied to either the process or the outcome. Are you are starting to empathize with the manager you thought was being unfair?

Whether the fairness of the process or the outcome takes precedent and whether the formula is equality or equity will depend on the nature of the decision. Where you are trying to strengthen teamwork and connection, an equal distribution of the outcome can be useful. Profit sharing is a common method for rewarding an entire group for the successes they have achieved through collaboration. Where you're hoping to spur individual performance, you can emphasize an equitable process. Sales incentives and other individual bonus payments encourage individuals to put in the maximum effort. Let the goals of the situation dictate which formula you use.

Even once you invest considerable effort in deciding fairly, that's no guarantee that your team will perceive it that way. Don't make the mistake of assuming your decisions will speak for themselves. If you are focusing on an equitable process for choosing who gets promoted, where you will weigh certain competencies or styles more positively than others, make your intentions known to your people. If you're emphasizing an equal sharing of the bonus pool to reinforce the importance of every member of the team, be up front about it.

Regardless of how you choose to make tough calls, it's critical that you communicate what you're thinking. Transparency increases trust and has value for your employees above and beyond the specifics of the decision-making process.

In the end, we all learn that life isn't fair. As a manager, you'll learn this much sooner than others. You'll face difficult choices where no resolution seems ideal and where the outcome will be perceived as fair by some and unfair by others. Don't be too hard on yourself. As long as you have thought carefully about what the business needs and made your assessment of the best answer as objectively as possible, you have done your job. You will always have an opportunity to restore balance with the next decision.

Liane Davey is a team effectiveness adviser and professional speaker. She is the author of *The Good Fight* and *You First*, and coauthor of *Leadership Solutions*. Follow her on Twitter @LianeDavey.

NOTE

1. Kees van den Bos, Riël Vermunt, and Henk A. M. Wilke, "Procedural and Distributive Justice: What Is Fair Depends More on What Comes First Than on What Comes Next," *Journal of Personality and Social Psychology* 72, no. 1 (1997): 95–104.

CHAPTER 20

Why People Challenge Your Decisions and What to Do About It

by Robert M. Galford, Bob Frisch, and Cary Greene

Leaders strive to be decisive. But all too often their well-reasoned decisions are reopened by bosses and colleagues or, worse, ignored, which slows down progress and breeds resentment, confusion, and paralysis. How

---

Adapted from "Why Decisions Get Second-Guessed, and What to Do About It," on hbr.org, February 25, 2016 (product #H02P06).

can you make sure that your decisions stick? In the course of researching our book, *Simple Sabotage*, we identified three of the most common reasons why they don't and pinpointed actions you can take to ensure that people follow the plan you've set out.

Reason 1: "You didn't ask me!"

Upon hearing about the decision, someone balks, claiming they weren't consulted. Maybe they disagree with the decision; maybe not. But they're upset they weren't brought into the process, and want to reopen the discussion. This can happen easily when an organization is growing, and decision-making rights have been delegated across a larger number of people. The question is whether the person should have been involved. Sometimes he or she needn't have been. But, if important stakeholders (especially those implementing the decision) were excluded, that's a problem.

The fix

Clarify the decision-making process. Take a lesson from Persian king Cyrus the Great, who said, "Diversity in counsel, unity in command." In other words, make sure to get enough input from the right stakeholders before making a decision. We're not suggesting you include everybody, but typically the more people you consult, the stronger their support will be, even if things don't go in their favor. Take advantage of one of the many good models out there (chapter 2 provides one such example) to help you define various roles and responsibilities from start to finish. Be sure to consult with those who might have objections to get their point of view, and include a representative of the team that will carry out the decision once it's made. Then, if someone says, "You didn't ask me," you'll be ready to explain why he or she wasn't included and why all those who made the decision were.

Reason 2: "I didn't tell you before, but I'm telling you now."

Someone who wasn't ever confident about the decision decides to speak up after it's been made. These late-breaking contrary views sometimes come from senior team members, who figure they should allow others to be heard and kill ideas only when and if they need to, which is often too late in the process. In other cases, junior people aren't confident enough to offer dissenting opinions in the moment.

The fix

Establish a new ground rule at the onset: "Silence denotes agreement." If those consulted about a decision don't say anything when it is being discussed, they are supporting it. No one—even a powerful team member or friend—can later say, "I'm not so sure."

Reason 3: "I know we agreed to something, but I'm going to implement something different."

This is probably the most insidious of the three: someone who originally agreed with the decision but now wants to recant their consent and execute something different *after* the fact. This typically happens when executives charged with executing on a plan go back and talk to their team members, who often have their own thoughts to add. The team then takes the liberty of making some changes in implementation, effectively altering the decision, with or without the knowledge of those who made it.

The fix

First, identify the person accountable for execution and make sure he or she understands the intent and specifics of the decision and the importance of following through on it completely. Second, create a timeline with explicit milestones: the date the decision will be made, the date it will be communicated to anyone affected, the date it will begin to be implemented, and the date that implementation is expected to be completed. Third, establish periodic checkpoints to make sure you're progressing in the right way.

In any situation, when a decision is questioned, you'll need to weigh the costs and benefits of reopening the decision versus staying the course. Reconsidering or revoking a decision for the wrong reasons slows down your organization and plants the seeds of an indecisive culture. In some cases, there may be valid reasons to rethink an agreed-upon plan, so you need to be able to differentiate. One quick test is to ask whether any new and relevant facts have come to light since the choice was made. Perhaps the price of the supplies you opted to buy has gone way up or someone has realized that the numbers you used were inaccurate or incomplete. If so, you might need to revisit your decision. But in the absence of new facts, you should heed the words of Admiral David Farragut: "Damn the torpedoes, full speed ahead!"

Robert M. Galford, managing partner of the Center for Leading Organizations, is the coauthor of *The Trusted Advisor, The Trusted Leader,* and *Your Leadership Legacy.* **Bob Frisch** is the managing partner of the Strategic Offsites Group, a Boston-based consultancy. He is the author of *Who's in the Room?* and four *Harvard Business Review* articles, including "Off-Sites That Work." **Cary Greene** is a partner of the Strategic Offsites Group and coauthor of the *Harvard Business Review* article "Leadership Summits That Work." He writes frequently for hbr.org. Galford, Frisch, and Greene are the coauthors of *Simple Sabotage: A Modern Field Manual for Detecting and Rooting Out Everyday Behaviors That Undermine Your Workplace.*

CHAPTER 21

Stop Second-Guessing Your Decisions

by Carolyn O'Hara

You've finally made a decision. Time to cross it off your list and move on. Or not? Do you find yourself revisiting every decision you make, agonizing over whether it really was the right one?

What the Experts Say

Everyone has moments of doubt. But "constant second-guessing can really affect your leadership—and the perception of your leadership among other people," says

---

Adapted from "Stop Second-Guessing Your Decisions at Work," on hbr.org, November 6, 2015 (product #H02H3K).

Sydney Finkelstein, faculty director of Dartmouth's Tuck Center for Leadership and the author of the book *Super-bosses*. It can also do unintended harm. "If you are excessively second-guessing a hire you've made, for instance, you are actually reducing the likelihood of that hire being successful," says Finkelstein. "There is a risk of a self-fulfilling prophecy." And that's not all. "Second-guessing also has a real productivity impact," says Amy Jen Su, cofounder of executive leadership development firm Paravis Partners and coauthor of *Own the Room*. "When you're spinning on a decision, you're not moving forward. You're just sitting in this purgatory of second-guessing."

Here's how to stop looking back with regret.

Get some perspective

Ask yourself: How big a decision was this really? What are the stakes now? "There are a lot of decisions where the costs of being wrong are actually not that big," says Finkelstein. If you're juggling other more important decisions and issues, "why spend another minute wondering about the 'what ifs'?" he says. "Remind yourself that worrying is taking time away from the bigger things you have to deal with." That exercise alone can help soothe your anxiety.

Check your gut

If you initially aren't feeling confident about a chosen path, don't discount where your intuition has led you. "Trusting your gut can be absolutely useful, valuable, and appropriate," says Finkelstein. "It can cut down on a ton of time." Both Finkelstein and Su suggest maintaining a kind of "acknowledgment practice," which might involve keeping a journal of recent decisions. Hopefully, you'll find that your intuition has led you in the right direction over time and that even when you made mistakes, they were easily corrected. Reviewing decisions in this way should help you become more self-assured, reducing the likelihood that you'll second-guess needlessly.

Poll a group of "advisers"

If checking your gut still doesn't give you the confidence that you've made the right choice, ask around for advice. "Have a group of people who are your sounding boards" and seek their input, says Su. "Say, 'Here's what I was thinking. What am I not taking into consideration here?' That will help you better understand what it is that's causing you to worry." It can be particularly helpful to stock this informal panel with people who have experience dealing with similar issues or who can bring new perspectives to the table. Their wisdom can help you feel more comfortable with your chosen path.

Get comfortable with adjustments

Few decisions are irreversible. But, in our quest to make the best ones, we tend to forget that. "There's a real tyranny to trying to be perfect," says Finkelstein. "It's important to remember that you can't possibly be right about everything." And in nearly every scenario, chances are "you can fix and adjust it," he says. Su agrees. "When we pretend that decisions are final, we paralyze ourselves. It's OK to make mistakes. Moving forward is what's important."

Make a date to check in

One of the best ways to stop questioning a decision in the moment is to make a plan to formally review it at a later date. It could be in a few weeks, or a few months—whatever feels appropriate. Add a reminder to your calendar. "The point is that you can set into place a very simple monitoring mechanism," says Finkelstein. "That greatly reduces the risk of the consequences of your decision going off-track, and you don't have to be so crazed in the meantime by second-guessing."

Balance your decision biases going forward

To protect yourself from second-guessing future decisions, work to step out of your comfort zone when making them. People tend to approach choices from either a subjective, emotion-driven perspective or an objective, logic-based one, says Su. But, to feel confident about a course of action, consider it from all angles: "If you are more logical and fact-based, stretch yourself to consider the subjective factors. If you're all about subjectivity, make sure you consider the logic side and marry the two."

Principles to Remember

Do:

- Trust your intuition.

- Reach out to a group of people for advice to put your mind at ease.

- Set a date to review the decision in the future so you can stop worrying about it in the present.

Don't:

- Sweat the small stuff. Recognize when decisions have low stakes.

- Assume the decision is permanent; you can almost always change course later on.

- Default to what makes you comfortable when making your next decision.

Case Study #1: Finding Confidence in Outside Advice

In 2007, when William Schroeder launched a boutique counseling center, Just Mind, in Austin, Texas, he knew that he'd have to make a deluge of daily decisions. But he found himself second-guessing many of them—big ones, like how many people he'd hired and clients he'd agreed to accept, but also small ones, like how much he was spending on Google AdWords campaigns. The worrying ate up his time and attention, leaving him drained. "It became the bane of my existence very quickly," he says.

Over time, he learned how to better insulate himself from needless doubt later on. In some cases, he creates a decision-making matrix to weigh his objectives and the factors in play. This helps him visualize his options, as well as reassures him that he's done enough research. "I am a visual person and being able to see my options helps me to feel more comfortable with a decision," he says. "It also allows me to have something to go back to and refer to later when I come up with a similar issue."

The other helpful tool he has developed is an informal group of advisers that he regularly polls when he needs reassurance and advice. He reaches out to another owner of a group counseling practice for hiring advice; to relatives like his psychologist father-in-law and his lawyer father; and to other entrepreneurs in the area for help running a small business.

"At the end of the day, you do the best you can and sometimes it doesn't turn out correctly," he says. "But if it doesn't go well, you try and fix it as quickly as possible and learn from it."

Case Study #2: When in Doubt, Move Forward

Matt Bremerkamp, VP of public relations for virtual assistant startup Pressed, was worried that he and his colleagues had made the wrong decision to expand the company's brand ambassador program. They'd gone back and forth over whether to cast a wide net with the program, which works with outsiders who evangelize the company's product, or shrink it, developing a smaller, targeted group of ambassadors. "We were debating the decision ad nauseum," he says.

To break through the inertia, Matt fell back on a strategy he had honed as an infantry team leader in the Army National Guard: Move left. "Basically, if after a moment of hesitation, a best course of action wasn't apparent, I would always have my team of men move left," he says. "Then I'd reevaluate the decision, and if a better course of action still wasn't apparent, we'd move left again, and so on." If left proved to be a poor choice, they'd change course. But "the point was to constantly keep moving forward and to never stagnate."

In this case, moving left meant implementing the decision to cast a wide net for brand ambassadors. "The decision actually ended up working out very well," Matt says. "Some of the issues that we thought we'd have, like relying on spokespeople that we hadn't handpicked or developed, really haven't come into play."

Matt says he now relies on the "move left" mantra all the time in his professional life. "A decision may not always be perfect," he says. "But by moving forward, you can always 'adjust fire' and redirect your efforts if need be."

———————

Carolyn O'Hara is a writer and editor based in New York City. She's worked at *The Week*, *PBS NewsHour*, and *Foreign Policy*. Follow her on Twitter @carolynohara1.

Managing Tough Situations

CHAPTER 22

When Your Team Always Struggles to Reach Consensus

by Bob Frisch and Cary Greene

The tension in the room was rising. The group had been at it for hours. In fact, this same team of 12 had been through essentially the same discussion on three previous occasions but still couldn't reach a decision on a critical issue: *Should the organization divest its South American operation or shift to a different strategy?*

Adapted from "A Good Meeting Needs a Clear Decision-Making Process," on hbr.org, March 5, 2019 (product #H04TSP).

They reviewed the pros and cons of both options yet again. Each side paraded their own experts, data, and recommendations. And yet they remained at an impasse.

This type of team indecision isn't uncommon. When a group of people need to come to an agreement on a difficult problem, it can be challenging to get everyone on the same page—especially when strong emotions and opinions come into play. What should you do when your team is tasked with making a decision or recommendation but struggles with reaching consensus? The solution is to plan ahead.

In our 60+ years of combined experience working with boards and senior executives at organizations ranging from *Fortune* 10 multinationals to German *Mittelstand* companies, we've seen leaders give plenty of thought to the data and analysis needed to kick off and carry on these sorts of discussions. But they typically don't consider how they'd like to finish them.

We're not suggesting they should know in advance *what* decision will be made. But before discussions even begin, they should know *how* a decision will be made if people can't agree.

In situations where everyone in the room reports to a common manager, and that person is present, there's not much of an issue. If the team can't decide, the boss will. But in today's highly matrixed organizations, closure in the absence of consensus can be an enormous challenge. Team members—even an individual executive—may well have multiple reporting lines. Finding a "natural tiebreaker"—whether one person or another group—may involve decisions bumping up two or even three levels, which is an impractical solution in many cases, and one that risks casting an unfavorable light on the group.

When we ask our clients, "What's going to happen at the end of the conversation if the decision isn't obvious? How exactly will it be made?" the answers often include: "Let's see how it goes," "We'll figure it out," or the classic "We'll cross that bridge when we come to it."

We think that's a bad idea. Your team shouldn't try to make an important decision unless everybody understands what's going to happen if its members can't reach an agreement.

So, before a decision-making meeting starts, be crystal clear about *how* the decision will be made. For example, tell the group there will be 90 minutes of discussion, and if there is no resolution after that time, the issue will be put to a vote. While this may seem obvious, be sure to consider how the results will be used. Does the verdict rest directly on the vote, or is the vote merely advisory for the accountable executive? Most decision-making models suggest that one person be accountable for making the final call, but if your organization takes a more collaborative approach, you need to clarify what a vote means. If it determines the decision, what is required? A simple majority? A two-thirds vote? Is anyone given veto power? (To learn more about establishing decision-making roles, see chapter 2.)

Also consider what happens if the executive or team with final authority isn't in the room. How should the issue get elevated? Will the vote be enough input? Should majority and minority viewpoints be documented? If so, how?

Once you've outlined a plan, share it with key stakeholders early so they can ask questions or suggest changes. It doesn't have to be complicated. In fact, it should be clear and simple so that everyone understands the process.

Early in his career, Tom Wilson, now chairman, president, and CEO of The Allstate Corporation, used to end each major meeting with a simple chart. For each significant decision, there were three boxes: "Yes," "No," and "Defer." Under the latter, there was space to indicate the date to which the issue would be deferred and what additional actions or data were required to move to a "Yes" or "No" at that time. This helped drive clarity and closure and made his meetings more efficient and decisive.

Teams don't need to get stuck spinning around a whirlpool of indecision. But by planning in advance how choices will be made, your team meetings can start with everyone clear on how they will end.

Bob Frisch is the managing partner of the Strategic Offsites Group, a Boston-based consultancy. He is also the author of *Who's in the Room?* and four *Harvard Business Review* articles, including "Off-Sites That Work." **Cary Greene** is a partner of the Strategic Offsites Group and coauthor of the *Harvard Business Review* article "Leadership Summits That Work." He writes frequently for hbr.org. Frisch and Greene are coauthors of *Simple Sabotage: A Modern Field Manual for Detecting and Rooting Out Everyday Behaviors That Undermine Your Workplace.*

CHAPTER 23

How to Choose Between Bad Options

by David Maxfield

Imagine this: You're a general manager for a manufacturing company and orders are up. You know you should be celebrating, but instead, you feel gut-punched. Your plants are facing severe capacity and material constraints, and you know you can't fill these orders. Now you must decide which ones to fill, which to delay, and which to turn away.

Your decision will favor winners and losers: desperate customers, angry sales reps, and frustrated factory

---

Adapted from "How to Get People to Accept a Tough Decision," on hbr.org, April 19, 2018 (product #H04AGG).

employees. And, if you don't get it right, your reputation with all of these stakeholders will take a serious hit.

Here's another tough decision scenario: You were just told that you've been laid off. It's not entirely surprising since your company—and the community you live in—has been struggling. Do you stay in your depressed community where your kids go to school? Or do you move to another state where jobs are more plentiful?

This decision is full of bad options and a good dose of uncertainty. If you move, you'll incur expenses and may even lose any unemployment benefits you're receiving. If you stay, you'll be in the same boat as your neighbor who has been out of a job for two years.

All leaders have to make tough decisions that have consequences for their organizations, their reputations, and their careers. The first step to making these choices is understanding what makes them so hard. Alexander George, who studied presidential decision making, pointed to two features:

- **Uncertainty.** Presidents never have the time or resources to fully understand all of the implications their decisions will have.

- **"Value complexity."** This is George's term to explain that even the "best" decisions will harm some people and undermine values leaders would prefer to support.

The decisions that senior leaders, middle managers, frontline employees, and parents must make often have the same features. Uncertainty and value complexity cause us to dither, delay, and defer, when we need to act.

What steps can leaders take to deal with these factors when making decisions?

Overcoming Uncertainty

Our initial reactions to uncertainty often get us deeper into trouble. Watch out for the following four pitfalls:

- **Avoidance.** It often feels as if problems sneak up on us when, in reality, we've failed to recognize the emerging issue. Instead of dealing with problems when they begin to simmer, we avoid them—and even dismiss them—until they are at a full boil. For example, perhaps your plants have been running at near capacity for a while, and there have been occasional hiccups in your supply chain. Instead of addressing these issues, you accept them as normal. Then, "suddenly," you're unable to fill orders.

- **Fixation.** When a problem presents itself, adrenaline floods the body and we fixate on the immediate threat. In this fight-or-flight mode, we're not able to think strategically. But focusing exclusively on the obvious short-term threat often means we miss the broader context and longer-term ramifications.

- **Oversimplification.** The fight-or-flight instinct also causes us to oversimplify the situation. We divide the world into "friends" and "foes" and see our options as "win" or "lose" or "option A" or "option B." Making a successful decision often requires transcending simplifications and discovering new ways to solve the problem.

- **Isolation.** At first, we may think that, if we contain the problem, it'll be easier to solve. That's rarely the case. For example, it may feel safer to hide the problem from your boss, peers, and customers while you figure out what to do. But as a result, you may wait too long before sounding the alarm. And, by then, you're in too deep.

To avoid these pitfalls—or to get out of them once you've fallen into them—it's best to take incremental steps forward without committing to a decision too quickly. The following are five things you can do to reduce uncertainty as you evaluate your options:

- **Assess the situation.** First, fairly consider and add up the risks of *not* acting. Seeing these costs will push you out of avoidance. Second, consider the pluses and minuses of your options. Walk through different scenarios to uncover hidden risks and discover new alternatives. For example, if you've lost your job, then not acting carries unacceptable risks. Moving to a high-employment area might make sense, but it comes with costs. Make lists of the costs and benefits of moving and not moving.

- **Don't get stuck.** Challenge any either/or assumptions you've made. Ask, "Can we do both?" and "What other options are available?" For example, can you focus your job search on a high-employment region without actually moving until you find a job? If you do find a job elsewhere, would it be possible to work remotely?

- **Add others' perspectives.** Grab a lifeline. Don't stew alone about the choices in front of you. Instead, talk to people you trust about the decision and your assessment. Chances are that if you expand your circle, you'll expand your options.

- **Try a test run.** Find a low-risk, small-scale way to test your alternatives. For example, if you can't fill all customers' orders, can you test having a few sales reps call select customers to delay orders and see what the response is? Can you outsource a few critical orders to another manufacturer? Use these tests to reassess the costs and benefits of your different options.

- **Take a step.** Break a complex decision into simple steps. Determine the very next step you need to take and then take it. For example, the next step is not: "Move to Omaha." Instead, it might be: "Call three recruiting firms in Omaha."

Overcoming Value Complexity

When you know that your decision is going to negatively impact others—say, hurt loyal customers or punish well-intentioned sales reps—watch out for the following missteps:

- **Don't downplay the damage.** When you have to make trade-offs, it's tempting to ignore or underestimate the damage. While this may make you feel better about your decision, it usually adds insult to injury for the person on the receiving end.

For example, if you decide to move, which means pulling your daughter out of her high school during her senior year, it's important to recognize the sacrifice she will make, not minimize it by trying to convince her it won't be so bad.

- **Avoid dehumanizing labels.** It's also easy to view your decision as picking winners and losers and then to disparage the "losers." For example, if you decide to fulfill certain customers' orders and delay others, you might try to make yourself feel better by saying that those who are getting delayed orders aren't valued customers anyway because they don't always pay on time or they order less. This may make it easier to stomach the harm you've caused, but it compromises your values. Instead, recognize and honor the stakeholders who must bear the brunt of your decision.

When a decision will result in unwanted harm or force you to compromise your values, use the following approaches to reduce the damage:

- **Make your intention clear.** Be as clear as possible about your intention. Explain that you are in a bad situation where any choice you make will harm someone. You don't wish negative consequences on anyone, but it's impossible to avoid.

- **Mitigate or compensate for the harm.** Find ways to make the people who were harmed feel whole again. Give them preferential treatment in the future to restore a sense of fairness, or give them opportunities to make up for what they have lost. For example, if some of your salespeople will lose the commissions from the sales you need to cancel, allow those canceled sales to still count toward their bonuses.

- **Minimize the maximum harm.** Humans tend to catastrophize and, when presented with bad news, imagine and obsess over whatever those worst-case possibilities might be. If you can anticipate these worst-case scenarios and take them off the table—honestly guarantee they will never happen—you can help to quell fears.

- **Recognize sacrifices.** When your decisions result in harm for some, frame the harm as a sacrifice they're making for the greater good. Their willingness to "take one for the team" should count in their favor. Do your best to turn them into heroes.

Decisions—whether they're about your business or your career—are often complex and, given the rate of change in the world, are getting more so. However, if you explicitly recognize the role that uncertainty and value complexity play in making these decisions difficult, you can take steps to ensure you're making the best choices with the information you have—and you can help those affected by your decisions better accept the consequences.

David Maxfield is a *New York Times* bestselling author, keynote speaker, and leading social scientist for business performance. He leads the research function at VitalSmarts, a corporate training and leadership development company. His work has been translated into 28 languages, is available in 36 countries, and has generated results for 300 of the *Fortune* 500.

CHAPTER 24

What to Do When You've Made a Wrong Decision

by Dorie Clark

It can be painful to admit when you've made a bad decision. Maybe you hired the wrong person, took a job that wasn't a good fit, or launched a new product line that no one seems to want. It's human nature to be optimistic and assume that success is just around the corner.

Eventually, as the ominous evidence mounts, you may start to doubt your idea. But it can feel overwhelming to admit the mistake in front of your colleagues and professional network. Here's what to do when you're starting to realize you've made the wrong choice.

Adapted from "What to Do When You've Made a Bad Decision," on hbr.org, August 11, 2016 (product #H032AB).

Recognize You Need to Act Quickly

Humans are highly susceptible to the sunk cost fallacy, which makes it hard for us to end something into which we've already put time, money, or effort. That's why many people stay in unhappy relationships ("But we've been together for five years already!") or hold onto losing stocks ("I bought it at $40 a share and I'm waiting for it to come back"), even when those prospects are dim. Similarly, you may have expended a great deal of political capital advocating for a geographic expansion, so it feels right to keep fighting for it until it proves successful. But if, rationally, it's never going to be successful, or will take decades to pay off and you need a much shorter timeframe, it's far better for your career to accept the loss now, rather than dragging it out and wasting even more resources.

Identify the Remedy

Sometimes a bad decision isn't a fatal one. You may have hired the wrong person for the job, but if she has the right attitude, she may be open to remedial training to get her skills up to par. You may have approved an expansion into Southern California that's floundering, but perhaps you can temporarily scale back to a Los Angeles County pilot to learn more about the new market. On the other hand, some problems require drastic and decisive action. If you absolutely hate your new job after a month, you may want to resign ASAP, so the company can make an offer to a qualified runner-up it spoke with during your recruitment process. It's essential to take a clear view of how to remedy your choice.

Extract the Lesson

Could you realistically have foreseen the problem? Sometimes, we're blindsided—you signed a lease just before a natural disaster struck, or company strategy changed dramatically right after you accepted a new job. But there are also plenty of bad decisions that, if we're honest, we could have prevented. Maybe you didn't vet the new job candidate carefully enough and relied on your gut instead of thoroughly canvassing her past supervisors and colleagues. Perhaps you overlooked growing signs of economic trouble and pushed ahead with the new line, despite knowing that luxury brands often struggle during a recession. Or maybe you didn't listen to your wife's qualms about relocating, and now it's escalated into a full-blown crisis. Making a bad decision is painful, but you can at least partially redeem it by learning from the experience. Take the time to understand where you went wrong. Were you too careless, or did you listen to unreliable sources, or were you blindly overoptimistic? Understanding your decision-making biases, and formulating a plan to overcome them, can help make you smarter next time. (Read more about the psychological traps that affect our decision making in chapter 1.)

Share the Knowledge

It's a lot easier to sweep bad decisions under the rug and pretend they never happened. But there's power in taking responsibility. When Jared Kleinert launched an online course—for which he promised partners $11,000 up front—and sold zero copies, that was a massive failure. But when he wrote about his experience publicly in an article on Forbes.com, dissecting the reasons behind his bad decisions and sharing those lessons with others, he changed the discourse. "The second I published it, everyone was saying how vulnerable . . . and transparent it was," Kleinert said when I interviewed him. "I think it attracts respect from people."

Unfortunately, making bad decisions is a part of life: No one has a 100% success rate. Even so, it's challenging to admit our mistakes in a culture that still often hides them. But when you do, and you work to remedy them quickly and honestly, you can mitigate the initial problem and earn the lasting respect of your peers.

Dorie Clark is a marketing strategist and professional speaker who teaches at Duke University's Fuqua School of Business. She is the author of *Entrepreneurial You, Reinventing You,* and *Stand Out.* Learn more at dorieclark.com.

CHAPTER 25

Make Good Decisions, Even When You're Short on Time

by Nick Tasler

In her *Harvard Business Review* article "Transient Advantage," Columbia Business School professor Rita Gunther McGrath describes how "fast and roughly right decision making will replace deliberations that are precise and slow." While most leaders couldn't agree more, the challenge is *how*? How do you know the difference between "roughly right" and "not at all right"? And just

---

Adapted from "Make Good Decisions Faster," on hbr.org, July 5, 2013.

how much time can elapse before "fast and roughly right" becomes "precise and slow?" Hours? Days? Months?

A simple, flexible know-think-do framework can enable leaders and their teams to immediately start making these fast and roughly right decisions. To paraphrase Einstein, this framework is "as simple as possible, but not simpler."

1. Know the ultimate strategic objective

The biggest hurdle to fast and roughly right decisions is criteria overload. Trying to weigh every possible objective and consideration from every possible stakeholder shoots the decision process in the foot before you even get off the starting line. Of the seven or eight possible objectives you would like to meet with this single decision, which one or two will make the biggest positive impact? Of all the possible stakeholders, which one do you least want to disappoint, and what is the objective they care most about?

2. Think rationally about how your options align with the ultimate objective

The vast majority of judgment errors can be eliminated simply by broadening our frame of reference. The quickest, easiest, most effective way to do this is by "consulting an anti-you" before you make every decision. As one banking executive explained, "It's amazing how many poor decisions can be avoided simply by asking one other person for their opinion." An impressive amount of empirical research backs up his observation. (The article "How Can Decision Making Be Improved?" published by

Perspectives on Psychological Science and spearheaded by Katherine Milkman of The Wharton School, provides an excellent summary.)

Consulting an anti-you works in two ways. The act of explaining your situation to another person often gives you new insights about the decision before the other person even responds. And the fresh perspective they offer in response is the second bonus.

3. Do something with that knowledge and those thoughts

After you've clearly defined the primary strategic objectives and laid out your research and thinking with one or two key anti-you's, it's time to call it quits on all of the planning, strategizing, number-crunching, and critical thinking. You simply must select one option, while letting go of all the other good options. It is helpful to remember here that in the real world, perfect options are a myth. Decision making will always be an exercise in coping with an unknowable future. No amount of deliberation can ever guarantee that you have identified the right option. The purpose of a decision is not to find the perfect option. The purpose of a decision is to get you to the next decision.

What makes the know-think-do framework particularly powerful for organizations ranging from tiny startups to behemoth banks and software makers is its scalability across every level of an organizational hierarchy. For example, a "fast and roughly right decision" might mean two weeks for the division heads at a *Fortune* 500 bank to decide how to remain competitive while also being compliant with a new government regulation. Or it might mean no more than 20 to 30 minutes for sales managers at the same bank's commercial lending team in Chicago trying to make a customer account decision.

Regardless of where you are or how big you are, this framework enables all corners of an org chart to share a common language and approach for making sound, timely decisions. So get started.

———————

Nick Tasler is an organizational psychologist, author, and speaker. Connect with him at NickTasler.com; follow him on Twitter @NickTasler.

Index

Engage with HBR content the way you want, on any device.

With HBR's new subscription plans, you can access world-renowned **case studies** from Harvard Business School and receive **four free eBooks**. Download and customize prebuilt **slide decks and graphics** from our **Visual Library**. With HBR's archive, top 50 best-selling articles, and five new articles every day, HBR is more than just a magazine.

Subscribe Today
hbr.org/success

Smart advice and inspiration from a source you trust.

If you enjoyed this book and want more comprehensive guidance on essential professional skills, turn to the HBR Guides Boxed Set. Packed with the practical advice you need to succeed, this seven-volume collection provides smart answers to your most pressing work challenges, from writing more effective emails and delivering persuasive presentations to setting priorities and managing up and across.

Harvard Business Review Guides

Available in paperback or ebook format. Plus, find downloadable tools and templates to help you get started.

- Better Business Writing
- Building Your Business Case
- Buying a Small Business
- Coaching Employees
- Delivering Effective Feedback
- Finance Basics for Managers
- Getting the Mentoring You Need
- Getting the Right Work Done

- Leading Teams
- Making Every Meeting Matter
- Managing Stress at Work
- Managing Up and Across
- Negotiating
- Office Politics
- Persuasive Presentations
- Project Management

Notes

Notes

Notes

Notes

Notes

Notes